KINGS & QUEENS
OF ENGLAND

KINGS & QUEENS OF ENGLAND

From the Saxon Kings to the House of Windsor

NIGEL CAWTHORNE

METRO BOOKS
NEW YORK

© 2009 by Arcturus Publishing Limited
This 2010 edition published by Metro Books,
by arrangement with Arcturus Publishing Limited.

Metro Books
122 Fifth Avenue
New York, NY 10011

ISBN: 978-1-4351-2136-2

Printed and bound in China

1   3   5   7   9   10   8   6   4   2

CONTENTS

INTRODUCTION

The kings and queens of England have always punched above their weight. They started out fighting for control of the southeast corner of England but it was not too long before they had taken over the remainder of the British Isles. Finally, they won the right to dominate a large proportion of the world.

At the height of the British Empire the nation's monarchs ruled over a quarter of the world's population and made their presence felt in many other parts of the globe. They have also made a great contribution to the establishment of common law, which forms the basis of the legal systems of the United States, Australia and India, as well as many other countries. And the Magna Carta, signed by King John in June 1215, guarantees freedoms that are cherished by much of the world. Britain's title to North America was created with the support of Henry VII (r.1485–1509), and the first English colonies were established under Elizabeth I (r.1558–1603). Although the American colonies were lost during the reign of George III (r.1760–1820), the British Empire continued to expand in India, Africa and the Far East. It reached its zenith during the long reign of Queen Victoria (r.1838–1901) whose upright family values perhaps shielded the British monarchy from the upheavals that toppled most other European dynasties.

Other English monarchs, such as Charles II – 'The Merry Monarch' – (r.1660–85), were not so virtuous, although his excesses were forgiven in the general relief that followed ten years of dour Puritan rule. His father, Charles I (r.1625–49), had been much less popular with the English people, but the fate of the latter extended the liberties of the British by establishing the precedence of the House of Commons. The reign of James II (r.1685–88), also came to an abrupt end but once again the British people were the beneficiaries, for the nation gained its Bill of Rights.

Even in this less than deferential age the respected figure of Elizabeth II has ensured that the monarchy still flourishes, although it is no longer the political centre of national life.

The Roots of Monarchy

England has been ruled by some 66 kings and queens over a period of around 1,200 years. Their reigns can be divided into ten dynasties, outlined in the chapters of this book (with the troubled reigns of the Houses of Lancaster and York cominbed into one chapter). The Anglo-Saxon Egbert of Wessex, who ruled from 802, was perhaps the first true English king, but legend has it that England had an earlier monarch, King Arthur. Arthur's story gained substance within the pages of *Historia Regum Britanniae*, a 'history' of Britain written by Geoffrey of Monmouth between 1135 and 1139. According to earlier chroniclers, Arthur led the Welsh – who arrived from the Continent in the Bronze Age – against the West Saxons who were advancing westwards from the Thames in the 6th century AD. This suggests that he was Welsh, not English. Others maintain that Arthur was not a king but a professional soldier, who commanded a cavalry force trained along Roman lines.

What we do know is that shortly after the Romans relinquished control of

Britain in AD410, a tyrant named Vortigern seized power. Instead of attacking Gaul in an attempt to turn himself into a Roman emperor, like earlier usurpers had done, he was content to stay in Britain. He gained allies by granting land to the Saxon people in Kent, who then aided him in his struggles against the Picts and the Scots who lived beyond Hadrian's Wall. However, the Saxons finally turned against him, which drove him to face them in battle. The two sides fought four battles in all, but Vortigern's army was severely weakened after the final conflict, in which he lost his son. Vortigern was forced to give the invaders even more land, this time in Sussex and Essex. It seemed that nothing

BELOW *This map of England during the 6th–8th centuries shows the kingdoms of the Saxon Heptarchy, which were gradually merged under one ruler.*

could stop the flood of Saxons, Angles and Jutes who came from the shores of Germany and Frisia, now part of the Netherlands.

The Britons halted the invaders at the Battle of Mons Badonicus in about 500, a victory that is associated with King Arthur, but by 550 the Germanic onslaught had begun again. By the end of the century the Britons had been forced back into the Welsh Marches and Dumnonia – the kingdom of Devon and Cornwall. Meanwhile, the invaders had crossed the Pennines and had advanced into Lothian.

However, the newcomers were not a unified force, because by AD600 they had established ten separate, though not necessarily independent, kingdoms. The word 'king' comes from the Old Frisian *cyning*, which means a tribal chieftain who is head of his kindred. The pre-eminence of seven of these kingdoms – Northumbria, Mercia, East Anglia, Essex, Wessex, Sussex and Kent – over the next 200 years gives this period its name: the Heptarchy. Northumbria was formed when Aethelfrith (r.592/3–616) united the kingdoms of Bernicia and Deira, before going on to defeat the Scots at Degsastan in 603 and the Welsh at Chester at some point between 613 and 616. Aethelfrith was then killed by Edwin (r.616–32), the exiled heir to Deira, who continued to hold the Welsh at bay. He became overlord of all Angle-land – England – except Kent, but after converting to Christianity he was killed at Hatfield Chase during a battle with Penda, king of Mercia (r.632–54) and Cadwallon, king of Gwynedd (r. 625–634).

At this point, Cadwallon was despatched by Aethelfrith's son Oswald (r.633–42), who retook Northumbria and became overlord to all the people south of the Humber. But under Penda

Mercia had been growing in power. After taking over the Severn Valley, following the Battle of Cirencester in 628, Penda defeated Oswald in 641 and drove the king of the West Saxons, Cenwalh (r.643–74), into exile in East Anglia, where he was forced to remain from 645 to 648. When Cenwalh returned to Wessex, Penda invaded East Anglia repeatedly, killing three of its kings. Then in 654 he invaded Northumbria, but he was defeated and killed by Oswald's successor, Oswiu (r.642–70).

Oswiu briefly became overlord of southern England, but a revolt in Mercia put Penda's son Wulhere (r.657–74) on the throne. Wulhere went on to become overlord of Surrey and Essex – and with it, London – before capturing the Isle of Wight. However, he overreached himself in 674 when he led the people of southern England in an attack on Northumbria – his army was annihilated by Oswiu's son Ecgfrith (r.670–85) and he lost his life. Ecgfrith was then defeated by Wulfere's successor Aethelred (r.674–704) at the Battle of the Trent in 679. He survived on that occasion but he was killed by the Picts in 685, after which Northumbria became a spent force. Caedwalla, king of Wessex (r.685–8), briefly came to prominence when he seized Surrey, Sussex, Kent and all the lands south of the Thames, but he quickly fell out of the equation when, in 688, he abdicated before travelling to Rome for baptism. He died in 689.

Caedwalla's successor Ine (r.688–726) issued a code of laws that became an appendix to the laws of King Alfred the Great. While Ine was spreading his kingdom westwards, Caedwalla's earlier gains in Surrey, Sussex and Kent were eroded and Wihtred (r.691–725) was able to establish the royal line of Kent. When Wihtred died and Ine abdicated – like

Caedwalla he went off to Rome – it left the way clear for Aethelbald, the king of Mercia (r.716–57), to take over and begin calling himself 'king of Britain'. Aethelbald was then murdered by his retainers and his cousin Offa (r.757–96) seized power. After building the great earthwork Offa's Dyke, a device to keep the Welsh out, he united the kingdoms of England. Offa's standing was such that he was able to forge diplomatic relations with Europe – he was treated as an equal by Charlemagne, king of the Franks (r.768–814) and Holy Roman Emperor (800–14), although the two later fell out. His silver coinage formed the basis of England's currency until the 13th century.

Offa died in 796 and his son died only a few weeks later, leaving their successor, Cenwulf (r.797–821), to face a revolt in Kent. After fighting an indecisive war against Eardwulf of Northumbria (r.796–806), who was later restored by Charlemagne, he died during an invasion of Wales, which left Mercia and Northumbria weakened and Wessex on the ascendant.

But things were changing, for Britons were leaving their old pagan ways behind. Christianity had been gradually taking over since Saint Augustine had landed in Kent in 597 and converted its king, Aethelberht (r.560–616). When Augustine became the first archbishop of Canterbury the new faith quickly began to spread. Northumbria became Christian in 685, Mercia soon put aside its heathen practices and there was a Saxon monastery in Exeter before 690. As the Church began to extend its power across the land, its influence helped unite England into a country that could be ruled by a single monarch.

ABOVE *Offa's Dyke was a great earthworks built by Offa, king of Mercia, to separate his kingdom from the lands of the Welsh. There was a ditch 12 feet (3.6 m) deep with a bank 18 feet (5.5 m) high on the English side.*

Alfredus Saxonum Rex.   Coll: Universitatis Oxon Fund:
        Circa A.   Chr. 872

Hujus summi Regis Effigiem   a Tabula in Bibl. Bodleiana factam
Reverendo Viro Nathan. Wetherell,   S.T.P. et istius Collegy Magistro, &c:
            Summa cum Humil: & Observantiâ D.D.D.   H. Parker.

CHAPTER ONE

THE SAXON KINGS

THE SAXONS

Egbert (802–39)

Aethelwulf (839–58*)

Aethelbald (856–860)

Aethelberht (860–5)

Aethelred I (865–71)

Alfred the Great (871–99)

Edward the Elder (899–924)

Athelstan (924–39)

Edmund I (939–46)

Eadred (946–55)

Eadwig (955–9)

Edgar the Peaceful (959–75)

Edward the Martyr (975–8)

Aethelred II, the Unready (978–1013, 1014–16)

Sweyn I (1013–14)

Edmund Ironside (1016)

Canute the Great (1016–35)

Harold I (1035–40)

Hardecanute (1040–2)

Edward the Confessor (1042–66)

Harold II (1066)

Dates show reign of monarch

* Overthrown from the throne of Wessex in 856

LEFT *The Saxon King Alfred was the only English king to get the honorific 'the Great' after his name, putting him in the same league as honoured figures of ancient times, such as Alexander the Great.*

The First Kings

Egbert, king of Wessex (r.802–39), is recognized as the first king of England because he put an end to the dominance of Mercia and Northumbria. He would go on to make Wessex so powerful that it would unify England under a dynasty that would be in existence for over 200 years.

Born in around 770, Egbert was the son of Ealhmund, king of Kent (r.784), who was a member of the royal family of Wessex. Offa took over the direct rule of Kent in 784 and Egbert was driven into exile on the Continent by Offa's son-in-law Beorhtric (r.786–802), his rival for the crown of Wessex. During his exile in France, it is thought that Egbert had dealings with Charlemagne – who had turned against Offa – perhaps even marrying one of Charlemagne's female relatives. When Beorhtric died – poisoned by his ambitious wife, according to legend – Egbert returned to Wessex to seize the crown.

ABOVE *Egbert, king of Wessex in the 9th century, can claim to be the first king of England, founding a dynasty that would unite the country.*

On taking the throne, Egbert took Wessex out of the Mercian federation and re-established it as an independent kingdom. Little else is known of Egbert's actions during the first 20 years of his reign, but in 825 he defeated Beornwulf, king of Mercia (r.823–5) at the Battle of Ellendune (now Wroughton in Wiltshire). Egbert claimed the crowns of Kent, Essex, Surrey and Sussex and was accepted by the people as their king. East Anglia also threw off the Mercian yoke with the slaying of Beornwulf. Seizing the opportunity, Egbert invaded Mercia and drove the new Mercian king Wiglaf (r.827–9 and 830–9) into exile. By taking control of the London mint he was then able to issue coins as the king of Mercia. Later that year, scribes began calling Egbert the 'ruler of Britain' because he now controlled all of the territory south of the Humber – while the Northumbrians, led by Eanred (r.810–40), had accepted his overlordship.

However, in 830 Wiglaf re-established himself as Mercia's ruler, although he failed to regain control of East Anglia and Egbert managed to hang on to the kingdoms of southeast England. But by this time a new enemy had entered the lists, because all of the kingdoms of England were being harried by the Vikings. Egbert was defeated by the Danes at Carhampton, west Somerset, in 836 but in 838 he won a great victory against the Vikings and their Welsh allies at Hingston Down in Cornwall, thereby ending the independence of the last independent English kingdom, Dumnonia.

Egbert then summoned the Council of Kingston in 838, at which he conferred lands and privileges on the sees of Canterbury and Winchester in return for their recognition of his son Aethelwulf (r.839–58). After that time, the churchmen crowned kings and wrote wills that specified the king's heir, thereby establishing the rule of the West Saxons. Egbert's line was now assured of a smooth succession. Winchester was established as the main city of Egbert's kingdom and after his death in 839 Egbert was buried there, followed by his son Aethelwulf, his grandson Alfred the Great and Alfred's son Edward the Elder.

THE VIKINGS

The Vikings, also known as Norsemen, were Scandinavian warriors who raided and colonized wide areas of Europe from the late 9th to the early 11th century. In their oar- and sail-powered longships, they travelled as far west as Iceland, Greenland, and Newfoundland and as far east as Constantinople and the Volga River in Russia. After a few early raids, attacks on England began in earnest in 865. The Vikings conquered the kingdoms of Northumbria and East Anglia and much of Mercia. But they were unable to subdue Alfred the Great, who further strengthened his position by negotiating a peace treaty in around 886, which recognized Danish rule in much of eastern England. However, Alfred's son Edward the Elder managed to reconquer the Danish-held territory. Viking raids began again in 980 and England became part of the empire of the Danish king Canute (r.1016–35). The Viking threat ended with the invasion of William the Conqueror, himself a Norman – that is, a descendant of the Norsemen who had settled in northern France.

RIGHT *Vikings set out in their longboats to attack Britain. They also settled in Normandy, Sicily and Greenland, and reached North America.*

Aethelwulf's first act as king was to give half of his kingdom – Kent, Surrey, Sussex and Essex – to his eldest son Aethelstan (r.839–c.855), keeping the western side of Wessex for himself. Then in 851 Aethelwulf scored a major victory over a large Danish army at a place called Aclea in Surrey. He then united the royal houses of Wessex and Mercia by marrying his daughter Aethelswith to the Mercian king Burgred (r.852–74) in 853, who went on to subdue the Welsh.

In 853, Aethelwulf sent his four-year-old son Alfred to Rome, before following on himself in 855, having left his kingdom in the keeping of his son Aethelstan. On his way back, Aethelwulf, now in his mid-fifties, married Judith, the 12-year-old daughter of Charles the Bald, king of the West Franks (r.843–77) and Holy Roman Emperor (875–7). But while he had been away Aethelstan had died and Aethelwulf's second son Aethelbald (r.856–60) had succeeded him. Aethelbald was part of a conspiracy to overthrow Aethelwulf and forced his father to abdicate the throne of Wessex in his favour. However, Aethelwulf remained king of Kent until his death in 858. On taking his father's throne Aethelbald also took his wife, marrying his 16-year-old stepmother, Judith, although the marriage was later annulled. When Aethelbald died, he was succeeded by his brother

ABOVE *Aethelred may have been defeated regularly by the Danes, but he handed the kingdom of Wessex intact to his brother Alfred.*

Aethelberht (r.860–5) who became king of Wessex and Kent. During his reign, the Danes attacked again, destroying Winchester in 860 and ravaging Kent in 865.

The next brother Aethelred (r.865–71) – sometimes called Aethelred I – succeeded in Wessex, though he does not appear to have been overlord of all of the disparate kingdoms of England. England was once more reeling under the constant onslaught of the Danes and in 865 a large Danish force landed in East Anglia, intent on conquest. Aethelred and his brother Alfred went to the aid of Burgred of Mercia when his kingdom was invaded, but the Mercians adopted the solution of buying the Vikings off.

After taking York the Danes then headed south, dealing Aethelred and Alfred a crushing defeat at Reading in

January 871. They struck back two weeks later, defeating the Viking army at a place called 'Aescesdun'. However, Aethelred was defeated again at Basing and at 'Maeretun' – possibly Merton in Surrey or Marden in Wiltshire. Aethelred died that Easter, perhaps from wounds sustained in battle, and he was succeeded by his brother Alfred the Great (r.871–99).

Alfred the Great

Born at Wantage, Berkshire, in 849, Alfred (r.871–99) was the fifth son of Aethelwulf and thus an unlikely candidate for the throne. Perhaps because of his early years in Rome, he was interested in scholarship. He was also a great admirer of Charlemagne, who had revived learning during his reign. However, there was little time for academic pursuits because England was under attack by the Vikings yet again. By the time Alfred took the throne at the age of 21, Wessex stood alone against the invaders.

Although they had been defeated at Wilton, the West Saxons had put up a fierce resistance against the advancing Vikings and Alfred had managed to negotiate a truce. Then in 876 the Danes began their onslaught again, but they were forced back in the following year. Finally, in early

RIGHT *The story of Alfred burning the cakes seems to have been entirely apocryphal. The idea behind it was that he was too preoccupied with matters of state to bother with domestic chores.*

878, the Danes made a lightning strike on Chippenham in Wiltshire, where they achieved their aim of creating a secure base from which to devastate Wessex. The Saxons submitted – with the exception of Alfred, who withdrew to the Somerset tidal marshes where he had probably hunted as a youth.

Alfred was given shelter by a peasant woman when he first fled to the Somerset Levels. Unaware of the king's identity, the woman asked him to keep an eye on some cakes she had left in the oven. However, the fugitive Alfred was so preoccupied with the defence of his kingdom that he forgot about the cakes.

THE ONLY ENGLISH KING TO BE CALLED 'THE GREAT'

Alfred is the only English king to have had the honorific 'the Great' added to his name. He was given the title in the medieval period, when his scholarly works were still being copied. For more than a thousand years he was seen as the 'great king' who maintained English independence against the Vikings. Another king of England has been called 'the Great' – Canute the Great. But he was a Dane.

Many other distinguished figures in history have had the title bestowed upon them. For instance, there was Herod, Constantine, Charlemagne, Catherine, Ramesses and Tamberlaine. And there have been two Peters and two Fredericks. It seems to come from the Persian title 'Great King', which was first used by Cyrus II, conqueror of Persia in the 6th century BC, although an ancient tablet claims that he was the 'son of Cambyses, great king, king of Anshan, grandson of Cyrus [I], great king of Anshan, descendant of Teispes…' All of the Persian kings that followed Cyrus took the title 'the Great'. That is, until the 4th century, when the Persians were overthrown by Alexander the Great – although a century or so went by before the title was affixed to his name. The Seleucid kings who succeeded Alexander also used 'the Great' as part of their personal names, as did the Roman leader Pompey. But other historical figures, such as Ashoka the Great of India and Hanno the Great of Carthage, were given the name posthumously.

RIGHT *Alfred the Great modelled himself on the Holy Roman Emperor Charlemagne and sought to bring literacy and law to his people.*

DANELAW

The Danelaw – Danelagh or Dena lagu – was the area of Anglo-Saxon England occupied by the invading Danish armies in the late 9th century. Its boundaries were formalized by the treaty between Alfred and the Danish warlord Guthrum in 886. Within those boundaries the Danes ruled the kingdoms of Northumbria and East Anglia and the lands of the five boroughs of Leicester, Nottingham, Derby, Stamford and Lincoln. As a result, the laws in eastern England between the Tees and the Thames differed from Mercian law to the west and West Saxon law to the south.

These differences persisted throughout the 11th and the 12th centuries, even when the Danes had been defeated. The Danes also left a large number of Old Norse words behind them, thereby making a great contribution to the growth of modern English.

When the woman returned and saw that her cakes had burned she took him severely to task. But that was before she discovered the identity of her visitor. Mortified, she stammered her apologies, but Alfred graciously assured her that he was the one who needed to apologize.

During his time in the marshes Alfred had been deciding on a plan of action, which was to build a fortified base at Athelney so that he could conduct guerrilla warfare against the Danes. Followers flocked from Wiltshire, Somerset and Hampshire and in May 878 Alfred's army defeated the Danes at the Battle of Edington. He then pursued them to their fortress at Chippenham where, after a two-week siege, they surrendered. Alfred soon realized that he could not possibly drive the Danes out of the rest of England, so he drew up a peace treaty which the Danes accepted. Under its terms the Danish warlord Guthrum converted to Christianity – with Alfred as his godfather – and became king of East Anglia (880–90). Guthrum's Danish subjects happily settled down as farmers and they even fought alongside Alfred when he faced a new Danish army that landed in Kent in 885.

Alfred then went on the offensive and seized London in 886, hoping that he could use the city as a springboard for the reconquest of the Danish territories. But he was not yet strong enough to do this, so he negotiated a new treaty with Guthrum which established the frontier of 'Danelaw' along Watling Street, the Roman road that ran from London to Wroxeter in Shropshire. The lands to the north and the east would belong to the Danes, while Alfred would secure West Mercia and Kent, along with Wessex.

At the same time, Alfred sought to build an alliance against the Danes by marrying his daughter Aethelflaed to the *ealdorman* – or chief magistrate – of Mercia. Alfred himself had married Eahlswith, a Mercian noblewoman, and another daughter, Aelfthryth, was married to the Count of Flanders, who represented a strong naval power at a time when the Vikings were settling in eastern England.

Alfred then reorganized his army with his *thanes*, or noble followers, and their men serving on a rota basis. In other words, they could tend their farms in times of peace but they could also be called upon as a rapid-reaction force if there was an attack. Starting from his capital at Winchester, he built a series of well-defended towns along the main river routes across southern England. They were so close together that no

CHARLEMAGNE THE GREAT

Born in 742, Charlemagne was king of the Franks from 768 until his death in 814. He expanded his kingdom into a Frankish superstate that incorporated all of Western Europe, with the exception of southern Italy, Asturias in northern Spain and the British Isles. This united the continent for the first time since the fall of the Roman Empire. When Charlemagne arrived in Rome in December 800, he was crowned Imperator Romanorum by Pope Leo III, a move that challenged the power of the Byzantine Emperor in Constantinople. His reign saw a revival of art, religion and culture through the medium of the Catholic Church. He was regarded as the founder of the French and the German monarchies and he is seen by many as the father of modern Europe.

ABOVE *Charlemagne united Europe and was crowned Holy Roman Emperor in Rome. Alfred the Great was sent to study in Rome soon after and tried, on a smaller scale, to emulate his idol.*

part of Wessex was more than 20 miles (32 km) from a fortress. Some towns were constructed on old Roman sites but others were completely new. They were called *burhs,* the Old English for fortress, from which comes the modern word 'borough'.

The loyalty of Alfred's army was purchased by handing out plots of land in return for manning the defences in times of war. He also maintained friendly relations with the Welsh, who even supplied him with troops in 893. Finally, he built larger and faster ships as a defence against coastal raiders. Although Alfred could make no further advances himself, he repelled another large Danish invasion in 892. The Danes kept on attacking until 896, but without any real success.

With the borders of his kingdom now secure, Alfred organized the country's finances. He also administered justice by drawing up a single legal code that incorporated the laws of Offa of Mercia, Ine of Wessex and Aethelberht of Kent, thereby creating the definitive body of Anglo-Saxon law. Another thing that made Alfred exceptional was his attitude to learning. He shared the contemporary view that the Vikings were a punishment from God because they had robbed England of many of its monasteries, the great medieval seats of learning. Alfred believed that only through knowledge could the English atone for their sins and live in accordance with the will of God, so he resolved to make up for the loss of the monasteries. One of the things he did was to found a monastery and a nunnery in an attempt to revive monasticism. He was also interested in architecture and art, and many European craftsmen were attracted to his court. Perhaps more importantly, he invited scholars from Mercia, Wales and the Continent to his palace and set about learning Latin himself so that he could translate books into English. He supervised translations of the Venerable Bede's *Ecclesiastical History of the English People* and *Seven Books of Histories Against the Pagans* by the 5th-century theologian Paulus Orosius. Then he personally translated *Pastoral Care* by Saint Gregory, the pope who sent Augustine to England, which became a handbook for priests, and the *Soliloquies* of Saint Augustine of Hippo. He was also patron of the *Anglo-Saxon Chronicle,* one of the greatest sources of information on Anglo-Saxon England. It began

OPPOSITE Edward's accession was resented by his stepmother Elfrida who wanted the crown for her own son Ethelred. When Edward was murdered while hunting, he was regarded as a martyr.

circulating soon after 890 and it was copied and supplemented up to 1154.

By the 890s, Alfred's charters and coinage referred to him as 'King of the English'. When he died in 899, at the age of 50, he left behind him a unified country that was strong enough to withstand further Danish onslaughts. He was buried in Winchester, the burial place of the West Saxon royal family.

Kings of all England

Alfred was succeeded by his son Edward the Elder (r.899–924), who built on his father's achievements and set about reconquering the lands held by the Danes. He began in 902 at the Battle of the Holme, where he defeated his cousin Aethelwald, the son of Alfred's elder brother Aethelred. Aethelwald was a rival claimant to the throne who had allied himself with the Danes, but he died in the battle alongside Eohric, king of the East Anglian Danes (r.890–902). Edward's next job was to thwart the Northumbrian Danes, and this he did by means of a resounding victory at Tettenhall in Mercia in 909. Following his father's example, he confined the Danes to the lands north of the Humber by constructing a new series of *burhs*.

That was still not enough for Edward. In 917 he combined forces with his sister Aethelflaed, ruler of Mercia (r.911–18), and overwhelmed the Danish army in East Anglia. Edward took over Mercia when Aethelflaed died in the following year and used it as a base from which to destroy the Danish armies in the Midlands. By the end of the year all of the Danes south of the Humber had submitted to him and in 920 he pacified Northumbria. By the end of his reign, the Norse, the Scots and the Welsh acknowledged him as 'father and lord'.

Edward's son Aethelstan (r.924–39), who had been brought up by his aunt

S. EDWARDVS REX ANGLIÆ, ET MARTI
Mart, 18.   M. bas.

Aethelflaed, achieved the complete political unification of England after 937 when he defeated Constantine II of the Scots (r.900–43), Owen of Strathclyde (r.c.915–37) and Olaf Guthfrithson, Norse king of Dublin (r.934–41) and claimant to the kingdom of York, at the Battle of Brunanburh. Five English or Irish kings and seven earls were said to have been killed on the Celtic side during the battle. Aethelstan also devised a code of laws to suppress theft and corruption, but he tempered justice with mercy, for the code contained provisions to mitigate the punishment of young offenders and bring solace to the destitute.

When Aethelstan died, Olaf Guthfrithson took the opportunity to seize Northumbria and invade the Midlands.

However, Aethelstan's successor, his half-brother Edmund I (r.939–46) – also known as 'Edmund the Deed-doer' or *'Edmundus Magnificus'* – regained the Midlands in 942, after Olaf Guthfrithson died. Then in 944 he retook Northumbria from Olaf Guthfrithson's successor, Olaf Sihtricson (king of York 941–4 and 949–51; king of Dublin 941–c.980) and Raegnald, king of York (r.919–20 and 939–44).

In 945 Edmund captured Strathclyde and entrusted it all to Malcolm I, king of Scotland (r.943–54), thereby beginning a policy of peaceful relations with the Scots in order to secure England's northern border. In the following year, Edmund was stabbed to death at the royal villa of Pucklechurch, in Gloucestershire, by an exiled robber named Liofa, who had returned to the court without permission.

Edmund I was succeeded by his brother Eadred

BELOW *The tomb of Alfred's grandson Athelstan, which can be found at Malmesbury Abbey. He is often regarded as the first king of England, unifying the country.*

(r.946–55). It was an unfortunate time because Erik Bloodax, king of Norway (r.c.930–35), was looking around for a new kingdom. He had succeeded to the Norwegian throne after the death of his father Harald I Fairhair (r.863–930) but two of his brothers had been left vassal kingdoms. He killed them both in an attempt to gain sole control of Norway but a third brother managed to eject him. So in 948 Erik seized Northumbria. Eadred managed to drive him out but the people of Northumbria then sided with Olaf Sihtricson. A fickle bunch, they deposed Olaf in 952 in favour of Erik Bloodax but two years later they sent Erik packing. He died in battle later that year and Northumbria once more fell to Eadred.

Eadred was not much more than 30 years old when he died of natural causes in 955. He had not married and so was succeeded by his 15-year-old nephew Eadwig (r.955–9), the eldest son of Edmund I. It is said that Eadwig disgraced himself at his coronation by leaving the banquet to debauch himself with a woman, possibly a close relative, and her daughter, 'a girl of ripe age'. When the monastic reformer Saint Dunstan sent Archbishop Oda after him, Eadwig was furious with the two men and he drove Dunstan into exile. He then married the woman's daughter, Aelfgifu, but they were separated by Archbishop Oda on the grounds of consanguinity. Eadwig's bad behaviour continued unabated when he stripped members of the royal family of their possessions, robbed the exchequer and issued some 90 charters. All of this caused such consternation that his kingdom only extended as far as the Thames when he died.

His brother Edgar (r.959–75) had already been made king of Mercia and Northumbria in 957 in place of Eadwig and at 16 years old Edgar became 'king of all England'. One of his first acts was to invite Saint Dunstan to return. He went on to found some 40 monasteries and he introduced penalties for the non-payment of tithes and Peter's pence, the annual contribution made by Roman Catholics to the Holy See. There was an absence of Viking raids during his reign, which earned him the title 'Edgar the Peaceful' – but that was a huge misnomer. According to the *Anglo-Saxon Chronicle,* he 'ordered all Thanet-land to be plundered' then took his army to

DANEGELD

Danegeld was the 'Danish tax' paid as tribute to Viking raiders in an attempt to save a country from their predations. The first payment of Danegeld was made in 845, when a Viking army threatened to attack Paris. The troops refrained from destroying the city when nearly 6 tons of silver and gold bullion was handed over. The English handed over 10,000 Roman pounds (3,300 kg) of silver in 991, following the Viking victory at the Battle of Maldon in Essex. Aethelred the Unready had been advised to bribe the Vikings rather than continue the armed struggle. In 994 the Danes returned and laid siege to London — the amount of silver they had previously received had simply convinced them that Danegeld was more profitable than plunder. Further payments were made in 1002 and 1007, when Aethelred bought two years' peace for 36,000 troy pounds (13,400 kg) of silver. In 1012, following the murder of the archbishop of Canterbury and the sack of the city, the Danes were pacified with another 48,000 troy pounds (17,900 kg) of silver. When Canute became king of England in 1016, he continued to levy Danegeld. In 1018, he collected 72,000 troy pounds (26,900 kg) of silver from the whole nation and a further 10,500 pounds (3,900 kg) of silver from London. This was used to decommission his invasion fleet, apart from the 40 ships that were retained as his personal bodyguard.

Chester where he humiliated six kings from Scotland, Wales and the Isle of Man by making them row him across the River Dee. He also strengthened the navy by employing a form of press-ganging.

Although he was ostensibly religious, in reality Edgar was sexually debauched. He married Ethelfleda Eneda, the daughter of his foster mother, when he was only 16 years old. Not content with

that, in 961 he imprisoned, seduced and impregnated a nun named Wulfrith. He appeared to see the error of his ways because he did not wear his crown for seven years, a penance suggested by Saint Dunstan. Perhaps the only good aspect of this sordid encounter was the birth of the child who would become Saint Edith, whose mother Wulfrith was also canonized. Wulfrith refused to marry Edgar after the death of Ethelfleda in 963, but the beautiful Elfrida caught his eye. They married in 965 after her first husband had been killed in a hunting

'accident', when a javelin thrown by Edgar had hit him in his back.

Edgar was succeeded by his son Edward (r.975–8), who was known as Edward the Martyr after he was murdered at Corfe Castle, probably by his stepmother Ethelfleda who lived there. Her 10-year-old son Aethelred II (r.978–1013 and 1014–16) then became king. Known as Aethelred 'the Unready', his epithet was really 'the Unraed', which means the ill-counselled. This is also a pun on his name because Aethelred, or Aethel-raed, means 'noble-counsel'. He

ABOVE *King Edgar receives the homage of eight princes in Chester. They rowed him down the river to show their loyalty before paying their tribute.*

23

was unpopular from the start because he did not seek to avenge his half-brother, or even bury him, and Edward was not interred until 980. However, Aethelred also suffered at his mother's hands for it is said that she beat him so hard with candles that he became conditioned to fear them.

There was a widespread belief that Aethelred might even have had a hand in the murder of Edward. Because of the resulting public unrest there was no unified defence when the Vikings started raiding again in 980. The country was ravaged, but efforts to pay the raiders off with Danegeld only made them more rapacious. When Danish incomers began settling in town, Aethelred had them massacred – which only succeeded in provoking more invasions. Sweyn Forkbeard, the king of Denmark (r.987–1014) and Norway (r.1000–14), led his marauding army in two punitive expeditions in 1003 and 1004, and when he returned in 1013, it was as Sweyn I (r.1013–14) – Aethelred was forced to seek shelter in Normandy. After Sweyn died, Aethelred's council of advisers invited him to return if he first settled their grievances.

Aethelred was succeeded by his son Edmund II (r.1016), but by that time Sweyn's son Canute was ransacking the country. Edmund was known as Edmund Ironside for his stout resistance to Canute's invasion but he defied his father by marrying the widow of a Danish lord in 1015. Edmund had been proclaimed king in London, but his position was seriously undermined by a large body of his nobles, who supported Canute. In a

ABOVE *Canute was the king of England, as well as Denmark and Norway, but his heirs could not manage to hold his empire together.*

bid to repel the usurper, Edmund laid siege to London and regained Wessex, but he was decisively defeated by Canute at Ashington in Essex. According to the ensuing peace treaty Edmund held Wessex while Canute took possession of all of the lands north of the Thames. Edmund died soon afterwards, leaving Canute as sole ruler of England.

The Danish Kings of England

Canute (r.1016–35) – also known as Canute the Great, Cnut or Knut – had accompanied his father on his conquest of England in 1013, but he was left to guard the fleet at Gainsborough, Lincolnshire. There he met Aelfgifu, the daughter of an *ealdorman* murdered by Aethelred the Unready, who bore him two sons, Sweyn and Harold. When his father died and Aethelred returned, Canute deserted his allies in England and set sail for Denmark, taking with him a number of hostages given to his father as pledges of allegiance. They were put ashore at Sandwich, horribly mutilated. He returned in 1015 with 200 longships and 10,000 troops, including the duke of Poland and a contingent of Slavs, and began a ruthless campaign against Edmund. When Earl Uhtred of Northumbria submitted to Canute, he was murdered in his hall for breaking his oath of allegiance to Sweyn Forkbeard.

Canute's first act as conqueror was to reward his Danish followers with estates that had been seized from the English. For instance, Viking chief Thorkell the Tall, who had taught him the arts of war, was given East Anglia and Eric of Hlathir acquired Northumbria. Prominent Englishmen, including Edmund's brother Eadwig, were either banished or murdered. However, Edmund's infant sons found refuge in Hungary. Canute then married Aethelred's widow, Emma of Normandy, who was the daughter of

TURNING BACK THE TIDE

Henry of Huntingdon, the 12th-century chronicler, relates that Canute set his throne by the seashore and commanded the tide to halt, so that his feet and robes would not get wet. When the tide failed to stop, Canute leapt back from the waves crying 'Let all men know how empty and worthless is the power of kings, for there is none worthy of the name but He whom heaven, earth, and sea obey by eternal laws.' He then hung his gold crown on a crucifix and never wore it again. This story is probably apocryphal because the contemporary *Encomium Emmae Reginae*, written for Canute's wife Emma, does not mention it, although other examples of Canute's Christian devotion are recorded. The Benedictine monk and biographer Goscelin, writing in the 11th century, recorded a different version of the episode. This time Canute placed his crown on a crucifix at Winchester one Easter, while declaring that the king of kings was more worthy of it than he. There is no mention of the sea. However, Henry of Huntingdon's story was repeated by later historians, who maintained that Canute staged the scene in order to rebuke the flattery of his courtiers. By showing them that the tides would not obey him he was demonstrating that he was a mere mortal. Canute was not the only historical figure to defy the tides. There are Celtic legends referring to the powers of Saint Illtud, Maelgwn, king of Gwynedd and Tuirbe, of Tuirbe's Strand, in Brittany.

ABOVE *The story of King Canute ordering the tide to stay back is well known. However, it can be interpreted either as an example of regal hubris or humility.*

Richard I of Normandy. This elevated his line above the heirs of England's overthrown dynasty. With an eye to the future, Canute nominated Harthacanute, his son with Emma, as his heir and sent him to Denmark to be brought up as a Viking. By doing this, Canute made sure that Emma's two sons by Aethelred, Alfred Aetheling and his younger brother Edward, were out of the running. They remained in exile in Normandy.

Canute became ever more English. He had an English wife and he began to fill his court with English nobles. In 1018, he paid off his fleet and the Danish contingent of his entourage diminished. At a conference in Oxford, Canute agreed to rule England 'according to Edgar's law'.

When his elder brother Harald II of Denmark (r.1014–18) died Canute went off to claim the Danish throne, supported by a bodyguard of English soldiers. Canute left Thorkell the Tall in charge of England but the two men fell out after his return in 1020. Thorkell was then outlawed, but the two men were soon reconciled, to the extent that Thorkell became regent for Canute's son Harthacanute (r.1035–42) in Denmark.

In 1020 Canute started laying claim to Norway, but he was faced by a combined force because Sweden had joined Norway in a coalition against Denmark. Although Canute seems to have been defeated at the Battle of the Holy River in 1026, the king of Sweden still made peace by ceding territory. The Norwegians fought on but in 1028 Canute drove Olaf II Haraldsson (r.1015–28) from the throne and placed Haakon, son of Eric Hlathir, in charge of Norway. After Haakon's death, Canute's concubine Aelfgifu and her son Sweyn took over, but they proved unpopular and were forced to flee to Denmark in 1035, before Canute's death. Olaf Haraldsson

ABOVE *Although Canute was Danish and spent little time in England, he increased the Baltic trade and strengthened England against the Scots.*

attempted to return in 1030, but he was killed at the Battle of Stiklestad.

Meanwhile, in 1027 Canute had made a successful expedition to Scotland to secure the fealty of the three Scottish kings. So when he travelled to Rome later in 1027, in order to attend the coronation of the German king, Conrad II (r.1024–39), as Holy Roman Emperor (r.1027–39), he was able to call himself king of Britain, Denmark, Norway and Sweden. Conrad's son Henry, later Henry III, married Canute's daughter Gundhilda in 1036, although she died soon afterwards. Nevertheless, Britain benefited from the union, because it strengthened Canute's control of Baltic trade.

Canute was succeeded by Harold I (r.1035–40), also known as Harold Harefoot, his other illegitimate son by Aelfgifu. Alfred Aetheling travelled hotfoot from Normandy in order to pursue his claim to the English throne, but he was captured and brought before Harold, who ordered his eyes to be put out. Unsurprisingly, Alfred died in the process. Harold then stripped Emma of Normandy of the treasures lavished upon her by his father and gave them to his mother Aelfgifu, who had returned to England. Emma was then exiled. The only person who could have helped her was Hardecanute, king of Denmark (r.1035–42), her son by Canute, but he did not feel able to leave his realm at that time. Nevertheless, he succeeded to the English throne (r.1040–2) when Harold died.

Harold was the first king to be buried in the abbey at Westminster, but this had little impact on Hardecanute who ordered his body to be exhumed and thrown into a bog. It is said that the corpse was later recovered and buried in a Danish cemetery in London, perhaps St Clement Danes. Hardecanute continued to make himself unpopular by introducing heavy taxes to pay for his fleet. When two of his tax collectors were killed in Worcester, he gave orders to devastate the county and kill all of its men, so Worcester was burnt and the shire was looted. Although Godwine, earl of Wessex had supported Hardecanute's claim when Harold had taken the throne, Hardecanute turned on him and had him tried over the death of his half-brother Alfred Aetheling. Godwine, who had been involved in Alfred's capture, swore that he had acted on Harold's orders. But he stayed alive by giving Hardecanute 'for his friendship' a ship with a gilded prow, crewed by 80 magnificently equipped men. Lyfing, bishop of Worcester, was also accused but he could not come up with such a bribe and so was murdered.

Hardecanute was not a well man and had neither wife nor children. In 1041, apparently fearing the worst, he sent to Normandy for his other half-brother Edward 'the Confessor'. His intention was to make Edward his official heir. On 8 June 1042 Hardecanute collapsed and died while drinking at a Viking wedding feast. He was just 24 years old.

Edward's Two Heirs

Edward the Confessor (r.1042–66) resented his mother Emma for having favoured Hardecanute, so when he came to the throne he seized her property. Much of Edward's long reign was peaceful and prosperous, apart from the odd skirmish with the Scots and the Welsh, but he had been in exile for 25 years and knew little of the country he sought to rule. He had been brought up at the Norman court, so it was natural for him to surround himself with his Norman friends. But this proved to be a source of considerable annoyance to the members of the houses of Wessex and Mercia, who had held considerable

power under the Danish kings. Nevertheless, in 1045 Godwine, the earl of Wessex, managed to marry his daughter Edith to Edward and so make himself the power behind the throne. But the two men fell out four years later. In 1051, with the support of Leofric of Mercia, Edward exiled the Godwine family and put aside his wife Edith.

Edward was already unpopular because of his Norman favourites, so when Godwine and his sons returned to England in 1052 they attracted a huge group of supporters. The king was forced to make terms. Godwine's lands were returned to him and many of Edward's Norman courtiers went into exile. When Godwine died later in the following year, his son Harold took over as the dominant power in the land. In 1063, he subjugated Wales and two years later he negotiated a settlement with the rebellious Northumbrians. Having dismissed his wife, Edward had no children so on his deathbed he named Harold as his successor. Edward died on 4 January 1066 and was buried in the new abbey he had constructed at Westminster.

Edward might have been a physical and political weakling but he was also seen as pious and unworldly. So much so that a cult grew up around him after the Norman Conquest. Almost a century after Edward's death the new king, Henry II, petitioned the pope to have Edward canonized, in a bid to gain the support of the English people.

In order to qualify for sainthood, a candidate must have been responsible for miracles. It was said that Edward had been the first monarch to cure people with scrofula, the 'king's evil', by his touch, so in 1161 he was duly canonized.

Despite his sainthood, Edward 'the Confessor' had presented Anglo-Saxon England with its greatest catastrophe. He had promised the crown to two people –

his protector, William the Bastard, duke of Normandy, and Harold Godwineson (Harold II). A bloody clash was inevitable. There was also another claimant – Harald III Hardraade, king of Norway (r.1045–66), who also disputed the throne of Denmark with King Sweyn II (r.1047–74). Harald's claim was supported by Harold's disaffected younger brother Tostig.

In 1055, Harold created Tostig earl of Northumbria, but his stern rule made him so unpopular that the Northumbrians rebelled. When Harold negotiated a peace with the rebels, Tostig headed for Normandy, where he offered his services to William the Bastard, who was related to Tostig's wife. After harrying the coast of the Isle of Wight, Kent and Lincolnshire – and possibly visiting Scotland and Norway – Tostig threw in his lot with Harald III. They sailed up the Humber and took York, but Harold II (r.1066) quickly marched his army north from London and surprised the Norwegians.

On 25 September Harold achieved a resounding victory at Stamford Bridge, where his army obliterated the Norwegians, killing Harald and Tostig in the process.

But Harold was going to meet a much greater foe on 14 October. The battle would cost him his crown and his life.

RIGHT *Edward the Confessor was buried in the church of St Peter, part of the new Abbey that he had built at Westminster.*

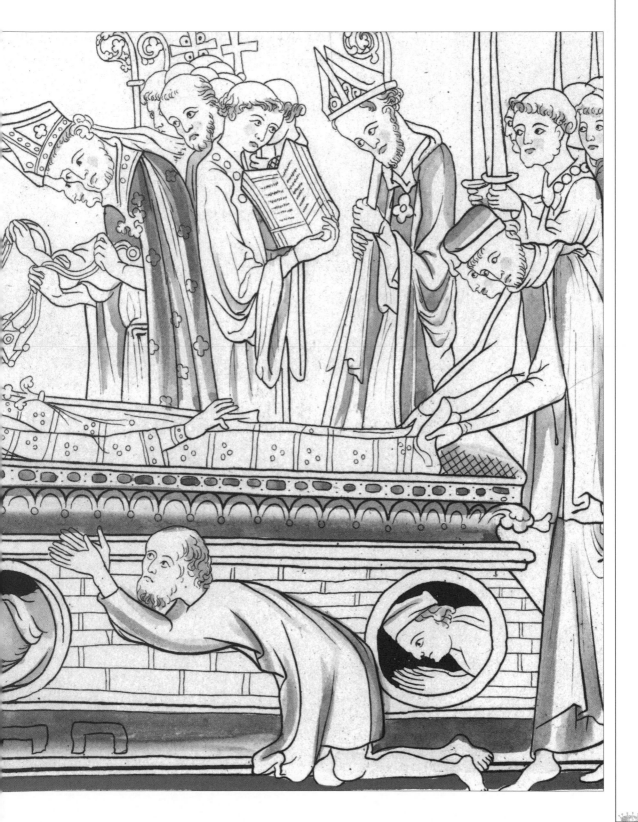

CHAPTER TWO

THE NORMANS

THE NORMANS

William I, the Conqueror (1066–87)

William II, Rufus (1087–1100)

Henry I (1100–35)

Stephen I (1135–54)

Empress Matilda (1141)*

Dates show reign of monarch

* contested the throne and was recognized as 'lady of England and Normandy'

LEFT *The Tower of London was built by William I to impose Norman rule on the capital. For centuries, it was the home of the monarch.*

William Conquers England

From time to time England has had a new dynasty thrust upon it. Although political and cultural turmoil is inevitable at such a time, the coming of the Normans was an especially traumatic event. England would be ruled by French kings for generations to come. The first of these kings was William the Conqueror, or William I (r.1066–87).

But William was a Norman rather than a Frenchman. The Normans, or Norsemen, were the descendants of the Vikings who had established a permanent presence in France in around 900. By 911, a Viking chieftain named Rollo was regularly besieging Paris. After a battle at Chartres, the French king Charles III the Simple (r.893–922) signed a treaty with the Viking intruder. Under the terms of the agreement Rollo was to give up brigandage, convert to Christianity and become Charles' vassal. In return, he was given lands around Rouen, which became the duchy of Normandy.

Born in around 1028, William was the illegitimate son of Duke Robert I of Normandy, the great-great-grandson of Rollo and Herleva, or Arlette, daughter of a tanner, or possibly an undertaker, who came from Falaise. Known as 'William the Bastard' to his contemporaries, his illegitimacy shaped

ABOVE *William the Conqueror was a great warrior, honing his skills as a young man in battles to hold on to the duchy of Normandy.*

his career. When his father died on his way back from a pilgrimage to Jerusalem in 1035, William succeeded him as duke of Normandy. Illegitimacy usually barred succession, so it is perhaps no surprise that some of his fellow Norman nobles became his bitter rivals. Three of his guardians and his tutor died violent deaths during his childhood. His great-uncle looked after the duchy during William's minority and his overlord, King Henry I of France (r.1026–60), knighted him at the age of 15.

From 1046 onwards, William successfully dealt with rebellions by his kinsmen and neighbouring nobles, all of whom questioned the right of a bastard to succeed. Then with the support of Henry I he began to expand his territory. But when William challenged Geoffrey Martel, count of Anjou, Henry took Martel's side. William was by now a hardened warrior and he held both of them at bay until they died in 1060 and were succeeded by weaker rulers.

In 1013, William's great-aunt Emma of Normandy, wife of Aethelred the Unready, sent her two children, Edward and Alfred Aetheling, into exile in Normandy. Apart from accompanying his brother on a brief foray into England in 1035, when Alfred was captured and killed, Edward remained in Normandy until 1041. For the final six years of his exile he lived under the protection of William.

In 1049, William began courting Matilda, daughter of Count Baldwin V of Flanders, who was descended from Aelfthryth, the daughter of Alfred the Great. The marriage was declared incestuous by the pope but the couple were so eager to marry that in 1053 they went ahead without papal approval. They were eventually reconciled with the pope in 1059 after building two monasteries in Caen. The marriage produced four sons and three daughters and in 1068 Matilda was crowned queen of England in Westminster Abbey.

William believed that Edward owed him the English throne in return for his earlier protection and support – marriage to a descendant of Alfred the Great had now greatly bolstered his claim. Even during his betrothal William had used his new alliance with Flanders as a means of putting pressure on Edward, who was by then king of England. Edward seems to have made some sort of promise in 1051. This might have been made in person. As we have seen, Earl Godwine had been exiled in that same year, together with his sons Harold and Tostig. According to one source, William visited England when his rivals were safely out of the way. But did Edward's intention to make William his heir lead to Godwine's exile? Or did Edward, fearful of the exiled Godwine's influence, make the promise in order to win allies on the Continent? The speculation continues. However, the promise only appears in Norman records, not in English ones.

That same year, Tostig Godwineson married the half-sister of Baldwin V of Flanders, making him William's uncle-in-law. Then in 1052 Godwine, Harold and Tostig returned to England. At a stroke, William's plans were thrown into jeopardy.

As it happened, William had other things on his mind at that point, because he was facing the powerful alliance of Henry I and Geoffrey Martel. With these two foes dead, William seized Maine in 1063. Shortly after that time he was joined by Harold Godwineson, then earl of Wessex. Harold had been sent to Normandy by Edward as an ambassador, but the exact nature of his mission is open to question. According to Norman sources it was to renew Edward's offer of the succession.

William did not expect to take England without opposition. In fact, he thought he might die in the attempt because in 1063 he named his son Robert as his heir. Norman rulers usually waited until the last months of their lives before they nominated a successor. When Edward died childless in 1066, William quickly sought the support of the pope. His invasion force was assembled under the papal flag. It took seven months for William to recruit around 7,000 Norman and French soldiers – up to 3,000 of whom were cavalry. On top of that, some 600 ships rode at anchor at the mouth of the Dives River near Caen. He planned to sail north, seize the Isle of Wight and then invade England by sailing through Southampton Water. But unfavourable winds kept the invasion fleet in port for a month, after which a westerly gale drove it up the Channel. The fleet re-formed at Saint-Valéry-sur-Somme, but there were more delays. Morale sagged in the cold and rainy conditions. Finally, on 27 September, a favourable wind propelled the fleet towards the southeast coast of England.

Prompted by the autumn gales, Harold had taken England's fleet out of service on 8 September, so the invaders made the crossing unopposed. William captured Pevensey before

BELOW *William I had his consort, Matilda of Flanders, crowned queen of England in Westminster Abbey.*

ABOVE *William I was victorious at the Battle Hastings. From there, he took London without further resistance.*

William had a further plan. He had been told that Harold had been fighting Harald and Tostig in the north, so his ploy was to force Harold to come to him. The English army would be exhausted after a 250-mile (400-km) forced march, but William's men would have had nine days in which to rest.

When Harold heard that William had landed he rushed his army south again and on the evening of 13 October the vanguard of his army emerged from the forest. But the main force did not arrive until dawn the next day. They were outnumbered, many of them were not professional soldiers and they had lost the element of surprise. On the positive side, they were formed up along the top of a ridge. The ground at the bottom was marshy and only a central strip was passable. From there, the French would have to attack uphill.

Using their shields as a defence against the French arrows, the English troops were able to cut down the first wave of infantry. At that stage, things were going less well for the French. Their cavalry attack was blunted by the slope. When they pulled back, the undisciplined English chased down the hill after them and the Norman line began to give. Then the rumour went round that William was dead and some Normans fled. Fearing that this might turn into a rout, William lifted his helmet so that his men could see that he was alive. This put heart back into his troops. They attacked and fell back in turns, keeping relentless pressure on the English line while giving themselves periods of rest.

The French designed tactics to lure the Englishmen down the hill to their deaths, but this also cost many Norman lives. By the evening, William knew he had to win that day or surrender. Harold would have reinforcements by the next day but he would have none. So he

dawn on 28 September, again without opposition. He had arrived at the head of the largest invasion fleet to land on British soil since the time of the Romans. It was so big that not all of the ships could fit into the tiny harbour, so most had to be beached towards the east. Added to that, the town itself was too small to hold William's troops. So two days later the Normans moved on to Hastings, where they raised fortifications. Hastings was a good choice for an invading army. Beyond Sedlescombe, which is close to Hastings, a Roman road led to Maidstone. From there, another road ran straight to London. But William was in no hurry to march on the capital. While his infantry was digging itself in, he sent his cavalry out foraging. William had a two-fold plan at this point. On the one hand he needed supplies for his army but on the other he wanted to harass the people of East Sussex. Harold was earl of Sussex, as well as Wessex, and William wanted it to appear that he could not defend his own people.

ordered an all-out assault. The archers fired high into the sky and the falling arrows thinned the English ranks. This shortened the wall of shields on the ridge, allowing the Normans to swarm up on the English army's flanks. But it took them a further two hours to scythe their way through to the spot where Harold had fallen, along with his brothers Gyrth and Leofwine. The retreating English staged a stout rearguard action at the edge of the forest, but they were cut down to a man.

Harold had held the crown for just ten months. There is no record of Harold's reign in the Domesday Book, though, so it seems that the Normans did not recognize it. The Bayeux Tapestry shows Harold being shot in the eye, but that was a symbolic death associated with perjury in medieval times. It was later claimed that by taking the crown Harold had perjured himself – hence the arrow in the eye. In reality, the cause of his death is unknown.

According to a Norman account Harold was buried overlooking the Saxon shore but others have maintained that he was interred at Waltham Abbey. However, both accounts could be wrong because recent research supports the notion that he was laid to rest at Bosham, his birthplace. There is a tale that Harold did not die at Hastings at all. According to the story, he spent two years recovering from his wounds in

BELOW *Battle Abbey in Sussex, as seen in 1906. It was founded by William the Conqueror to commemorate his victory at Hastings.*

Winchester before leaving for Germany. After spending many years wandering around Europe as a pilgrim, he returned to England an old man. Calling himself Christian, he spent ten years living as a hermit in a cave outside Dover. After that he travelled to Chester, where he once again became a hermit. Then, as he lay dying, he confessed that he had been born Harold Godwineson.

In 1070, as a penance, William had an abbey built on the site of the battle, with the high altar occupying the spot where Harold had fallen. The ruins of Battle Abbey, and the town of Battle which grew up around it, are still there.

BELOW *The 231 feet (70 m) of the Bayeux Tapestry provide a record of the Battle of Hastings and the events that ran up to it.*

Norman Rule Begins

William was crowned king of England on Christmas Day 1066. He was the first king to be crowned in Westminster Abbey. Fearing an assassination attempt, Norman soldiers set fire to the surrounding houses. Smoke filled the abbey and the congregation fled, but the coronation was completed despite the chaos. During his coronation William promised to uphold existing laws and customs: but there would be new laws also. Within weeks, the earls of Northumbria and Mercia had submitted to William. Three months later, after confirming the privileges of the city of

NEW LAW

At his coronation, William the Conqueror promised to uphold existing laws and customs. So the Anglo-Saxon shire courts and 'hundred' courts, which administered defence and taxation as well as justice, remained intact. He also allowed the regional variations in law created by the Danish invasion to continue.

However, William was a centralizer. In order to strengthen royal justice he replaced the small landowners who had previously been sheriffs with influential nobles. Their function was to supervise the administration of day-to-day justice in the existing county courts. But William sent members of his own court to conduct important trials. To complicate things further, he introduced church courts, which administered a mixture of Norman and old Roman law.

ABOVE *An accused prisoner is brought before a sitting of the Shire Moot, the forerunner of today's County Court.*

Another innovation was the introduction to England of 'Forest Law', which was widespread on the Continent. William's feudal lords had hunting rights, and the sole right to cut down trees, on the lands he gave them. The king himself was inordinately fond of hunting and he cleared large areas to make way for the chase, taking little heed of the villages and peasants in his path. One of the best testaments to William's passion for hunting is the New Forest, which was one vast royal deer reserve protected by royal writ. According to the *Anglo-Saxon Chronicle*:

'…whosoever slew a hart, or a hind should be deprived of his eyesight. As he forbade men to kill the harts, so also the boars; and he loved the tall deer as if he were their father. Likewise he declared respecting the hares that they should go free. His rich bemoaned it, and the poor men shuddered at it.'

These laws caused great resentment. In the eyes of English chroniclers the New Forest became a symbol of William's greed. Nevertheless, the king managed to maintain peace and order. In 1087, the *Anglo-Saxon Chronicle* explained:

'He was a very stern and violent man, so no one dared do anything contrary to his will… Amongst other things the good security he made in this country is not to be forgotten.'

ABOVE *Bishop Odo, the half-brother of William the Conqueror, commissioned the Bayeux Tapestry. He also had political ambitions of his own.*

London, he was feeling confident enough to return to Normandy. He left two regents in charge – Normans who had been newly ennobled as the earls of Wessex and Kent. The new earl of Kent was William's half-brother Odo, bishop of Bayeux, who was later to commission the Bayeux Tapestry. When William returned to England in December, the country was on the edge of rebellion. The regents had only been able to maintain control because of a programme of castle building. William began the wholesale confiscation of the estates of the English nobles, although it was mostly their heirs that lost out. Many nobles had died at Stamford Bridge and Hastings. These lands were given to William's Norman, French and Flemish allies in exchange for military duties, which included raising troops. By the end of William's reign, the king's tenants had acquired about half of England's landed wealth. Only two Englishmen still held large estates directly from the king. A French-speaking aristocracy had become the new governing class.

William created up to 180 'honours' – lands scattered throughout the shires, each with a castle as a governing centre. At any one time, he had some 5,000 knights at his disposal, who were able to repress rebellions and pursue campaigns. They were augmented by mercenaries and English infantry from the Anglo-Saxon militia – the cost was met from local levies. The king also maintained a royal army as a personal bodyguard.

In early 1068, Harold's sons raided the

southwest coast of England, but they were summarily dealt with by William's local commanders. William then took an army to subdue Exeter, where he installed a Norman castellan (local ruler). He did the same with Cornwall, this time leaving a Breton earl in charge.

But William's problems were not yet over. In 1069 Aethelred's grandson, Edgar

Aetheling, had joined forces with other English nobles and the Danes. Their objective was to invade the north and take York. William lost no time in marching his army through the Midlands and on to York. He symbolically imposed his authority on the ruined city by wearing his crown at a feast on Christmas Day. His next task was to drive the Danes back to their ships on the Humber. In order to avoid any further uprisings, William then moved on to devastate Northumbria and Mercia – an operation known as the 'harrying of the north'. His object was to deprive future Danish invasion forces of supplies and prevent the recovery of English resistance. Churches and monasteries were burnt and agricultural land was laid to waste, creating a famine that lasted for at least nine years. Sadly, the chief losers were the unarmed peasants. William then crossed the Pennines to put down revolts along the Welsh border. Castles were built at Chester and Stafford.

Returning to Winchester, William staged a second coronation, in which he was crowned by cardinals who had been sent by the pope. He then extended his authority over the Church. At the 1070 Council of Winchester English bishops were stripped of their offices and replaced with

BELOW *Warwick Castle, built by William the Conqueror in 1068. It was one of the many castles built by William to suppress any resistance to Norman rule.*

HEREWARD THE WAKE

Hereward the Wake was a symbol of Anglo-Saxon resistance to the Norman Conquest. Expecting an invasion by Sweyn II of Denmark (r.1047–74) in 1070, Hereward's followers and a band of Danish sailors sacked Peterborough Abbey, perhaps to keep its treasures out of the hands of a new Norman abbot. They took refuge on the Isle of Ely, then an island that rose above the surrounding fens. Soon afterwards Sweyn made peace with William I and the Danes returned home. The Isle of Ely then became home to a number of Anglo-Saxon fugitives, including the earl of Northumbria. In 1071, William besieged the island, taking it by building a causeway. Hereward escaped, but it is not known what happened to him after that. Later he became a hero of romantic fiction. It has been suggested that his epithet 'the Wake' signifies 'the wakeful one'. However, it is more likely that it derives from his supposed relationship with the manor of Bourne in Lincolnshire which, from the mid-12th century, belonged to the Wake family.

RIGHT *Hereward the Wake fought back against the Norman invaders. But resistance against the Conqueror was futile.*

Norman or French clerics. The cathedrals at Canterbury and Durham were rebuilt and some of the bishops' sees were moved to urban centres, where they could be controlled more easily. In the following year, William put down the final pockets of English resistance. Hereward the Wake made a last desperate stand on the Isle of Ely, but to no avail. William then marched on into Scotland, forcing King Malcolm III Canmore (r.1058–93), successor to Macbeth, to accept him as overlord. Malcolm was made to hand over his eldest son as a hostage and expel Edgar Aetheling from his court.

William consolidated his position by building castles at Warwick, Nottingham, York, Lincoln, Huntingdon and Cambridge. These were entrusted to William's loyal followers and their private armies. The new king was to build over 80 castles during his reign, including the Tower of London. These forts were of the motte and bailey type. A deep circular ditch was dug and the excavated earth was piled into the centre, forming the motte. Wooden towers were often erected on these mounds. Baileys were defensive areas adjacent to the mottes, protected by earth ramparts. Many of these structures were later rebuilt in stone, so that they became a permanent reminder of the new Norman feudal order.

After 1072 England was secure and William spent most of his time in Normandy and France. Here he was in conflict with Philip I of France (r.1060–1108), also known as 'Philip the Amorous' or 'Philip the Fat'. Philip sought to join forces with Edgar Aetheling by offering him a castle at Montreuil near Normandy's northeast border. Unfortunately for Edgar his fleet was wrecked by a storm in the North Sea on his way there. So the last Englishman with a claim to the throne

BELOW *William the Conqueror originally built a wooden motte and bailey castle at York. But resistance was stiff, so he replaced it with a stone fortification.*

was then forced to bow to the inevitable. After making his peace with William he returned to court. Philip then teamed up with William's named heir Robert, who attempted a rebellion in Normandy. William was understandably incensed, though father and son were later reconciled.

But William was rarely free from opposition. In 1075 Earl Waltheof, Ralph de Gael of Norfolk and Roger of Hereford, the last English earl, cooked up a half-hearted rebellion at a wedding feast. The plot is known as the 'revolt of the earls'. William left his deputies to put it down, returning to England only after he had been told that the Danes were

threatening to invade. The invasion did not materialize. That Christmas, William first attended the funeral of Edward the Confessor's widow Edith and then meted out harsh punishments to the rebels. Roger of Hereford had his hands cut off and spent a long period in prison and the others were mutilated and exiled. Waltheof threw himself on the king's mercy, but he was still beheaded.

In 1080, William returned to England after hearing that the king of Scotland had ravaged the north. However, when he arrived he sent his son Robert to deal with the Scots while he turned his attention to Wales, which he invaded in 1081. A year later, it was the turn of Odo,

BELOW *A page from the Domesday Book, an inventory of the lands in England conquered by William I.*

THE DOMESDAY BOOK

The 'harrying of the north' and the redistribution of landed wealth cause an economic slump – and there were expensive military campaigns to pay for. An increase in tax revenues was needed. This prompted William to order a full-scale investigation into the wealth of the kingdom. The scope, speed and efficiency of this survey was remarkable for its time. A panel of seven or eight commissioners, taking several counties apiece, carried out a detailed analysis of all of the estates of the king and his tenants-in-chief south of the Ribble and the Tees – 13,418 settlements in all, although some are marked 'wasted'. A summary was then compiled, which was called the Domesday Book. The name refers to 'doomsday' – when men face the record to which there is no appeal.

The book comes in two volumes. *Great Domesday* contains the final summarized record of all the counties except Essex, Norfolk and Sussex. This seems to have represented the extent of the work at the time of William's death in 1087. Unsummarized accounts of the other three counties appear in *Little Domesday*. The volumes are now on display in the National Archives in Kew.

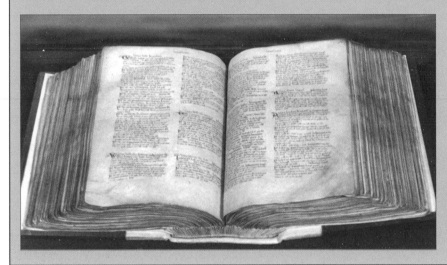

LEFT *Once an entire picture of England was collated in the Domesday Book, William could send his tax gatherers out.*

William's half-brother and regent. According to William's sources, Odo had not only been plotting to become pope by force or bribery but he was also planning to succeed William when he died. He was arrested for his pains.

Then in 1083 William's beloved wife Matilda died – she was said to be England's shortest queen at 4 foot 2 inches (130 cm) – and he fell out again with his son Robert, who remained in exile for the rest of William's life.

A growing Danish threat and fighting in France was draining William's exchequer, so he needed to raise money by taxation. From 1086 he began a survey of the wealth of the country, which was recorded in the Domesday Book. William took the opportunity to travel around the southern counties while the survey was being conducted. He then summoned all of his nobles to Salisbury, where each one of them was required to swear an oath of fealty directly to him. Until then, each noble had merely paid tribute to his particular overlord. Dubbed the 'Salisbury oath', it was William's way of ensuring that there would be no further rebellions.

William spent the last months of his life fighting a counter-offensive in Normandy. Philip I had annexed part of

ABOVE *A depiction of the heads side of a coin issued by William Rufus, son of William the Conqueror.*

the Normans' outlying territory and William was trying to regain it. He fell from his horse during the Siege of Mantes and it is thought that he injured himself on his saddle pommel. The ailing king was carried back to Rouen where he died on 9 September 1087. He was buried in the abbey church of Saint Étienne at Caen, which he had founded. His tomb was desecrated by Huguenots in 1562 and French Revolutionaries in 1793. So the burial place of the first Norman king of England is now marked by a simple stone slab.

The Dynasty Continues

When William I died he left Normandy to his eldest son Robert, despite their differences. His second son Richard had been killed in a hunting accident in the New Forest, so England was left to his third son William II, Rufus (r.1087–1100). His fourth son, Henry, was left £5,000 in silver.

The 'Rufus' part of William II's name refers to red hair or complexion – although one account mentions that his hair was blond. It is unlikely that William II was called Rufus in his lifetime. It seems that the epithet was added later, in order to distinguish him from his father. William Rufus was his father's favourite and he was probably responsible for the initial falling-out between William I and Robert. While campaigning in France, Rufus and his younger brother Henry paid Robert a visit. The two boys, it is said, went upstairs to play dice 'as soldiers do' but then they urinated on the heads of Robert and his friends. There was a fight and the king intervened, forcing the brothers to make up. But Robert felt he had lost face, so he rebelled. In the fighting that ensued both William Rufus and William I were wounded – the king was injured by Robert.

By 1080 Rufus and Robert had become reconciled. Rufus joined Robert in an expedition to quell the Scots and later accompanied his father on his foray into Wales. He fought alongside his father and his brother in Normandy, but he stayed with his father when Robert fell out with the king again in 1083. It seems that William I wanted to disinherit Robert completely but he was advised against it.

Many of the Norman nobles were unhappy about Rufus getting England and Robert inheriting Normandy. They owned land on both sides of the Channel and did not want to serve two masters. So they came up with a plan to unite England and Normandy under a single ruler. William's half-brother Odo of Bayeux, earl of Kent, was chosen to lead the revolt, the Rebellion of 1088, that would oust Rufus in favour of Robert. In the event, William managed to win the nobles over with promises of tax cuts and improved government. The rebellion

LEFT *Malcolm III Canmore, king of Scotland, swore fealty to William I, but soon broke his oath, making raids over the border into England.*

ABOVE *Henry I, the fourth son of William I and Matilda of Flanders, succeeded his unpopular brother William Rufus.*

failed and Odo fled to Normandy, where he became Robert's aide.

Rufus then reneged on his promises, provoking a second baronial revolt in 1095. This time he put down the insurrection with great brutality. One of the ringleaders, Count Guillaume of Eu, was blinded and castrated. Needless to say, he did not survive this treatment. Even the count's steward was hanged, while others were mutilated, imprisoned, fined or banished. No one dared defy William Rufus' authority again. He even attacked the church, seizing the lands of Canterbury. The archbishop, Saint Anselm, was forced to flee.

In 1093, William Rufus killed Malcolm III of Scotland when he rebelled. Afterwards he maintained the Scottish kings as vassals. Then in 1097 he subjugated Wales. But William's chief interest lay in wresting Normandy from his brother Robert. The siblings were locked in battle from 1089 to 1096. Hostilities ended when Robert mortgaged the duchy to William in order to raise money to go on the First Crusade.

William Rufus was a short man, thickset and muscular, with a protruding belly. Even so, he always dressed in the height of fashion, however outrageous it might be. He avoided marriage, preferring the company of men, and his court was a scandal.

As one dismayed cleric related:

'Then was there flowing hair and extravagant dress, and was invented the fashion of shoes with curved points; then the model for young men was to rival women in delicacy of person, to mind their gait, to walk with loose gesture, and half naked. Enervated and effeminate, they unwillingly remained what nature had made them, the assailers of others' chastity, prodigal of their own.'

It seems likely that these goings-on added to William's unpopularity. In 1100, he was shot in the back while hunting in the New Forest. He died from the wound. The man who fired the arrow, Walter Tirel, lord of Poix in Ponthieu, fled from the scene. Tirel was a fine soldier by all accounts, so many considered the incident to be an assassination rather than an accident. If so, perhaps Tirel was acting on the orders of William Rufus' younger brother Henry. Whatever the truth, Henry seized the throne before Robert could return from the Holy Land.

The First Henry

Henry I (r.1100–35) was crowned in Westminster Abbey, just three days after William II's death. By then Robert had barely reached Italy. However, Robert was popular among the Norman barons so Henry had to work quickly. First of all he issued the Charter of Liberties, which promised to end capricious taxes, the confiscation of Church property and William Rufus' other excesses. He also reorganized the legal system, sending royal justices out to tour the shires. Then he recalled Saint Anselm and secured the succession by marrying Matilda, daughter of Malcolm III of Scotland, whose mother Margaret was descended from the English royal line.

By the time Robert finally reached England in 1101, Henry had become popular with the people and the barons. Saint Anselm negotiated a settlement whereby Henry would retain England while Robert could rule Normandy, including Henry's own lands in France. He would also receive a large annuity. However, Robert was not a good ruler. Norman churchmen fled to England and begged for Henry's help, which gave him the opportunity to invade. But Henry was not just a rough soldier like his brother – he was a skilled politician. He bribed the Norman barons and made alliances with Normandy's neighbours. Henry then invaded Normandy in 1105 and 1106, finally defeating his brother at the Battle of Tinchebrai on 28 September. Robert remained a prisoner in Cardiff Castle until his death in 1134.

While Henry was posing as a champion of the Church in Normandy, he was fighting Saint Anselm in England. Anselm was attempting to introduce the reforms of Pope Paschal II, which were designed to put an end to lay investiture – that is, the sale of ecclesiastical appointments by the sovereign. Henry was understandably opposed to such a move, because the Church was a good source of revenue. Matters came to a head when Pope Paschal threatened Henry with excommunication. In the

end, Henry relinquished the right to appoint churchmen, but they would still owe him homage for their lands.

A skilled diplomat, Henry I married his daughter Matilda to Henry V of Germany (r.1099–1125), who was also the Holy Roman Emperor (1111–25). At the same time, he was grooming his only legitimate son William Aetheling as his heir. Henry then turned to Normandy, where he faced a new challenge from the imprisoned Robert's son William Clito, who was supported by Louis VI of France (r.1108–37). They were no match for him and he defeated them both at Brémule in 1119. His next task was to have his son William Aetheling

ABOVE *William Rufus was killed, whether by accident or intentionally, by an arrow from the bow of Walter Tirel in 1100.*

recognized as duke of Normandy and then married into the house of Anjou.

But William drowned in the following year, along with one of Henry's illegitimate sons, when the *White Ship* carrying them across the Channel sank. Henry I was now without an heir. He married Adela of Louvain, but the union proved childless. When Henry V of Germany died, Matilda returned to England where Henry made his barons pay homage to her as his heir. In 1128, she married Geoffrey Plantagenet, heir to Anjou. Five years later, she bore her first son, the future Henry II (r.1154–89).

RIGHT *Stephen I seized the throne when his uncle Henry I died. Henry had nominated his daughter Matilda to inherit.*

THE WHITE SHIP

The *White Ship* was owned by Thomas FitzStephen. His father Stephen had been sea captain for William the Conqueror when he invaded England in 1066. When, in 1120, Henry I was about to leave Barfleur for England, Thomas offered him the use of his vessel. The king had already made other arrangements but he suggested that his son William Aetheling might like to return in the *White Ship*. It was dark when the *White Ship* set off and its port side tragically struck a submerged rock. Operated by a crew who were more than likely drunk, the ship quickly capsized and sank. William got away safely but he insisted on returning to the wreck to rescue his sister, which caused his small boat to founder. The only known survivor was a butcher from Rouen. He was wearing thick ramskins that saved him from exposure and was picked up by fishermen the next morning.

William Aetheling, the only legitimate son of King Henry I of England, was not the only important person to die. William of Malmesbury wrote:

'Here also perished with William, Richard, another of the King's sons, whom a woman without rank had borne him, before his accession, a brave youth, and dear to his father from his obedience; Richard d'Avranches, second Earl of Chester, and his brother Otheur; Geoffrey Ridel; Walter of Everci; Geoffrey, archdeacon of Hereford; [Matilda] the Countess of Perche, the king's daughter; the Countess of Chester; the king's niece Lucia-Mahaut of Blois; and many others… No ship ever brought so much misery to England.'

Civil War

Matilda was in Anjou when Henry I died in 1135, while Henry's nephew Stephen of Blois was in Boulogne. Stephen had promised to recognize Matilda as the lawful heir to the English throne, but when the time came he hurried to London and claimed the crown for himself. He was crowned Stephen I (r.1135–54) at Winchester by the archbishop of Canterbury and with the encouragement of his brother, Henry de Blois, bishop of Winchester. Shortly afterwards the Norman barons accepted Stephen as duke of Normandy. He further secured his position by a successful appeal to Pope Innocent II.

While Stephen had won the support of almost all of the Anglo-Norman bishops and magnates, there were sporadic uprisings in favour of Matilda. Her uncle, David I of Scotland (r.1124–53), attacked across the border and the Welsh also made incursions.

In 1139 Matilda led an invasion that unleashed a bitter civil war. After a series of victories, Stephen was captured in a battle at Lincoln in 1141 and Matilda was accepted as 'lady of England and Normandy'. Stephen's cause might have been lost had not Matilda's haughty manner provoked a rebellion among the citizens of London, where she had gone for her coronation. Matilda found it necessary to leave London for Oxford.

A combination of mismanagement and unpopularity led to Matilda losing her advantage. Stephen was exchanged for Robert, earl of Gloucester, Matilda's half-brother, who had fallen into the hands of the king's supporters. Matilda herself was captured but she famously escaped from Oxford Castle over the frozen Thames in December 1142. The war continued with no conclusion in sight. Then, in 1148, Matilda was forced out of England, retiring to Normandy until her death in 1167.

CHAPTER THREE

THE PLANTAGENETS

THE PLANTAGENETS

Henry II (1154–89)

Richard I 'the Lionheart' (1189–99)

John I (1199–1216)

Henry III (1216–72)

Edward I (1272–1307)

Edward II (1307–27)

Edward III (1327–77)

Richard II (1377–99)

Dates show reign of monarch

LEFT *The head of the Welsh prince Llywelyn ap Gruffydd was paraded through the streets of London on a pike after he died in battle in 1282.*

The First Plantagenet King

Henry II (r.1154–89) was born at Le Mans in 1133. The son of Matilda, daughter of Henry I and Geoffrey Plantagenet, count of Anjou, Maine and Touraine, he was educated partly in England. In 1150 he became duke of Normandy and when his father died in the following year he assumed the title of count of Anjou. He further advanced himself by marrying Eleanor of Aquitaine, who had recently divorced Louis VII of France (r.1131–80). Louis then tried unsuccessfully to crush Henry, who in just two years had moved from being a landless wanderer to the most powerful man in western France. But his acquisitions did not stop there.

In January 1153, Henry invaded England in pursuance of his mother's claim to the throne. There were a number of clashes. King Stephen found his support ebbing away, but fought on in the hope of securing the succession for his son Eustace. When Eustace died in August of that year Stephen lost heart and signed a treaty with Henry. This allowed Stephen to continue as monarch, but named Henry as his heir.

Henry II came to the English throne in 1154 – he was the first in a line of fourteen Plantagenet kings. The dynasty would last for more than 300 years. He was short and stocky with legs slightly bowed from endless days on horseback and his hair was reddish, although he kept his head closely shaved. But his blue-grey eyes were his most distinctive feature. They were said to be 'dove-like when he was at peace' but 'gleaming like fire when his temper was aroused'.

Henry spent his life travelling around his possessions, which stretched from the Solway Firth to the Pyrenees. Although he reigned for 34 years he spent just 14 of them in England. The marriages of Henry's three daughters had also given him influence in Germany, Sicily and Castile. In addition to that, Pope Adrian IV (in office 1154–9), the only English pope, gave Henry the right to rule Ireland. He obtained the homage of the Scottish kings, took Northumberland

ABOVE *Henry II ruled England and much of France, but he is remembered for the murder of Thomas à Becket.*

THE HOUSE OF PLANTAGENET

Henry II and his royal descendants are referred to as the House of Anjou or the Angevin dynasty. Plantagenet was not the surname of Henry's father, Geoffrey V, count of Anjou, but it was instead a nickname. Some say he was dubbed Plantagenet because he liked to wear a sprig of broom (or *Planta genista* in Latin), others suggest that he planted broom to improve his hunting covers. However, the nickname did not become a hereditary surname. His descendants in England remained without a surname for over 250 years, even though surnames became universal for non-royals.

Some historians suggest that only Henry II and his sons Richard I and John I should be known as the Angevin kings while their descendants, particularly Edward I, Edward II and Edward III, should be called Plantagenets. But the only occasion on which the name Plantagenet was used officially was in 1460, when Richard, duke of York, claimed the throne as 'Richard Plantaginet'.

back from them and invaded Wales. However, all of his achievements were overshadowed by his quarrel with Thomas Becket, known to history as Thomas à Becket.

Becket was a low-born city clerk who rose to become Henry's chancellor from 1155 to 1162. He was a brilliant administrator as well as being a leading figure at court. He oversaw the repairing of the Tower of London, he brought castles down, he conducted foreign affairs and he raised and led troops. Above all, he was Henry's closest friend. As such he enjoyed wealth and the trappings of high office. At the time, Henry and the Church were engaged in a battle for supremacy, so Henry came up with a plan. He would appoint someone who would do his bidding as archbishop of Canterbury – his faithful friend Thomas.

Against all expectations, Becket took this new role seriously. First of all he became devout and then he resigned the worldly office of chancellor. Even worse, he opposed Henry's new taxes and excommunicated a leading baron. But the conflict came to a head over the matter of ecclesiastical jurisdiction. The Church had long asserted its right to try miscreant clergy in its own courts, where they could be punished by demotion or exile but not mutilation or death. On the other hand, the king claimed that he had the authority to try all criminals, including clergy, in his own court. In 1164, Henry passed the Constitutions of Clarendon, which spelled out the relations between the Church and the State. Becket and the bishops verbally agreed to the Constitutions. But the archbishop then changed his mind and appealed to the pope.

Henry demanded that Becket be tried for breaching his feudal obligation. Realizing that the king was out to ruin him, Becket went into exile in France.

Henry countered by seizing Becket's property and banishing his relatives, while the archbishop responded with threats of excommunication. In 1169, the two men met in Montmirail, but negotiation failed and they parted in bitterness.

The king then extended the Constitutions of Clarendon, thereby

BELOW *A depiction of Thomas à Becket, the archbishop of Canterbury who excommunicated the king and paid the price.*

ABOVE *According to tradition, Thomas à Becket was killed by four knights in Canterbury Cathedral. Within days his tomb became a place of pilgrimage and he was canonized three years after his death.*

denying all papal authority in England. He followed that by having his son Henry, the 'Young King', crowned by the archbishop of York, rather than by the archbishop of Canterbury. In response, Pope Alexander III (in office 1159–81) and Becket jointly excommunicated Henry and his followers. Fearing that they might interdict the whole country, Henry met Becket at Fréteval and invited him to return to Canterbury.

Becket resumed his role as archbishop of Canterbury to popular acclaim, but refused to lift the excommunications. When he heard this, Henry exclaimed, 'What miserable drones and traitors have I nourished and promoted in my household, who let their lord be treated with such shameful contempt by a low-born clerk!' By oral tradition, this was translated into, 'Who will rid me of this turbulent priest?'

Four knights interpreted Henry's outburst as a royal command. They sped from Normandy to England and, late in the afternoon of 29 December 1170,

confronted Becket in Canterbury Cathedral. In the ensuing struggle Becket was hacked to death by the knights' swords.

When Henry heard of Becket's murder, he went into seclusion for three days. Clergy all over Europe were outraged – Pope Alexander refused to speak to an Englishman for more than a week. England was interdicted and Henry closed the Channel ports and fled to Ireland, only returning in 1172. His journey began the English annexation of the island. Then in May 1172 the king met Alexander III's legates at Avranches, where he submitted to their judgment. He admitted that his words might have prompted Becket's murder, even though he had never desired his death. Kneeling in contrition, he acceded to the demands of the Church. The episode became known as the Compromise of Avranches.

Although she was 11 years older than her husband, Eleanor of Aquitaine gave Henry five sons and three daughters, with all but one of their sons surviving into adulthood. The four surviving sons – Henry, Geoffrey, Richard and John – quarrelled due to Henry's habit of ostensibly dividing his possessions among his sons while in fact reserving real power for himself. Even as his co-regent, his son Henry the Young King had no real power. However, he had been betrothed to Louis VII's daughter Marguerite since the age of five, which

LEFT *Eleanor of Aquitaine bore Henry II eight children, but was imprisoned by him in 1173 for supporting her sons' rebellion. On Henry's death in 1189 she was finally released, and lived for a further 15 years.*

reduced the rift between Henry and Louis. Marguerite's dowry would be Gisors and the Vexin. With a special dispensation from the pope, they were married two years later. In 1172, Marguerite was crowned queen consort of England.

Henry the Young King fell out with his father when the king tried to find territories for his fourth son John, at the expense of his brother Geoffrey. John was Henry II's youngest son and his favourite. He was betrothed to Alys, the daughter of Humbert III, count of Maurienne (Savoy), but because of his brothers' rebellion he did not get the territories he needed for the marriage to go ahead. Accordingly, he became stuck with the nickname 'Lackland'.

The rebellion grew when Richard backed his two elder brothers, followed by Eleanor. It was supported by numerous barons and the kings of Scotland and France. Henry II defeated them one by one over the next year. Although Henry became reconciled with his sons, he imprisoned Eleanor in 1173. She remained in custody until his death in 1189. In 1174, not long after Eleanor's imprisonment, Henry's liaison with the 'Fair Rosamund' – Rosamund Clifford – became public knowledge. The chronicler Gerald of Wales wrote that Henry

'…having long been a secret adulterer, now openly flaunted his mistress, not that rose of the world [*Rosa mundi*] of false and frivolous renown, but that rose of unchastity [*Rosa immundi*]'.

Henry provided for John in 1176 by organizing his betrothal to Isabella of Gloucester. Isabella's father, the earl of Gloucester, had died without a male heir and it was arranged that his titles and wealth should go to Isabella – and so to John.

There were further disputes among the princes. Richard had inherited Aquitaine at the age of 11, so it is no surprise that he rebelled when Henry II gave it to Henry the Young King. When Henry died in 1183 Aquitaine was passed to John, which spread further discord among the brothers. In 1185 Henry also gave John the lordship of Ireland.

Geoffrey allied himself with Philip II Augustus of France (r.1179–1223), who had succeeded his father Louis. However, after boasting that he and the French king were going to devastate Normandy, Geoffrey died in an accident at a tournament in Paris in 1186. Richard then became Philip's ally and, it is thought, his homosexual lover. Together they defeated Henry II, who died at Chinon on 6 July 1189, after

BELOW *Rosamund Clifford, the long-term mistress of Henry II, believed to be the mother of two of his illegitimate children.*

THE CRUSADES

By the end of the 11th century, around two-thirds of the ancient Christian world had been conquered by Muslims. It was Pope Urban II who first put forward the idea of a holy war that would recapture Jerusalem and other Christian territories. The First Crusade, in 1095–9, was successful in establishing four small Christian states in the Holy Land – the kingdom of Jerusalem, the County of Edessa, the Principality of Antioch and the County of Tripoli. That was followed by the Second Crusade, in 1147–9, which was a response to the Muslims' recapture of Edessa. The Crusaders made no further gains in the Middle East, but they regained Lisbon in Portugal from the Muslims and slaughtered a number of Jews in the Rhineland.

In 1187, the Muslim leader Saladin retrieved Jerusalem, prompting Pope Gregory VIII to call for a Third Crusade (1189–92). Several monarchs eagerly stepped forward – Philip II of France, Richard I of England and Frederick I, king of Germany (r.1152–90) and Holy Roman Emperor (1155–90). Poor Frederick sadly drowned crossing a river, so he never got there. But although the crusaders defeated the Muslims at Arsuf and retook Jaffa, Jerusalem eluded them.

The Fourth Crusade (1202–4) was ill-funded and it ended with the crusaders sacking

ABOVE *A depiction of Richard I advancing to Jaffa during the Third Crusade, where he defeated Saladin and took the city.*

Constantinople, the Byzantine capital. This resulted in the final split between the Roman Catholic Church and the Eastern Orthodox churches. Beginning in 1209, the decade-long Albigensian Crusade was closer to home. It sought to purge heresy from southern France. This was followed by the Children's Crusade, in 1212, in which some 37,000 children were said to have been led into the fray. According to the records none of them actually reached the Holy Land. Many died or were sold into slavery along the way.

Despite all of this, the European appetite for retaking Jerusalem and recovering the True Cross continued to run high. The Fifth Crusade (1217–21) was aimed at Egypt, which was seen to be the centre of Muslim power. After some initial successes it foundered. Frederick II (r.1220–50) had more success in the Sixth Crusade (1228–9). He managed to force the sultan of Egypt to relinquish control of most of Jerusalem, although the Dome of the Rock and the Al-Aksa Mosque remained in Muslim hands.

In 1243, the occupying army was defeated by a force of Khwarezmian tribesmen and Jerusalem was once again lost. In response, Louis IX of France (r.1226–70) mounted a Seventh Crusade (1248–54) against Egypt. It failed and Louis was captured and ransomed. He died in Tunisia on the Eighth Crusade in 1270.

The Ninth Crusade (1271–2) was undertaken by the future Edward I of England. It was a complete disaster because all of the remaining crusader states fell after that point. The last Christian foothold, the island of Ruad 2 miles (3.2 km) from the Syrian shore, was held by the Knights Templar until 1302, when it fell to the Mamluks.

hearing that John had joined his enemies. Richard had harried his dying father until he had named him as his heir. He became duke of Normandy on his father's death and was crowned king of England two months later. One of his first acts was to release his mother.

The Crusading King

Although Richard I (r.1189–99) is one of England's most famous kings, he had little English blood in him, did not speak the language and spent only ten months of his ten-year reign in the country. He regarded his realm as little more than a source of revenue for his crusades. 'I would have sold London itself if I could have found a rich enough buyer,' he said. Many towns benefited from the royal charters he gave them in return for their financial assistance.

Henry II had promised to undertake a crusade in order to expiate the murder of Thomas Becket. He also had another motive in that the Angevins had acquired the title to the crusader kingdom of Jerusalem by marriage. Unable to acquit his pledge, Henry bequeathed it to Richard, whose prowess on the battlefield earned him the sobriquet *Coeur de Lion* ('Lion-Heart' or 'Lion-Hearted'). Richard's reputation had been gained because of the ruthlessness with which he had put down revolts in his French possessions. In 1179 he even seized the castle of Taillebourg in Saintonge, which was thought to be impregnable.

When Richard took the throne it was shortly after Saladin's capture of Jerusalem in 1187, and preparations were being made for the Third Crusade. Richard was determined to join, but first

he needed to secure Normandy and Anjou. Open war against France was averted when Philip II also decided to join the crusade. As soon as Richard had raised an army, he headed for the Holy Land, leaving England in the hands of his mother, the newly freed Eleanor of Aquitaine. She was to defend Richard's interests against the intrigues of his brother John.

Richard planned to winter in Sicily on the way to the Holy Land but he found the Sicilians inhospitable. So he took Messina by force, making his nephew heir to the Sicilian throne by marrying him to the king's daughter. He also invaded Cyprus. On 8 June 1191, after landing in Palestine with his ally Philip II of France, he joined the siege of Acre (now Akko in Israel). Although the conflict had been in progress for two years, Richard moved quickly. Within six weeks he had defeated the Muslim defenders, taken the city and put 2,700 prisoners to the sword.

Richard then welded the multinational crusaders into a single force. He marched them down the coast to a point at which they could be supplied by ship. They travelled in battle order, in three divisions of three columns. Saladin's horse-borne archers constantly harassed the troops, but they were defended by Richard's crossbowmen.

On 7 September 1191, Saladin attacked in force at Arsuf. Richard kept the crusaders on the defensive for most of the day, repelling attack after attack. Then when the Muslim forces were tiring, the Master of the Knights Hospitallers suddenly charged. Richard ordered the whole crusader force to surge forward, taking the Muslim army by surprise. The rout was complete. Richard's troops were so disciplined that he was able to prevent them from chasing the fleeing Muslim soldiers, who tried to lure the crusaders into the desert. Saladin lost 7,000 men but only 700 crusaders perished.

Saladin left scorched earth behind him as he retreated towards Jerusalem. Richard was far from the coast and his ships so he could no longer supply his men. He was forced to abandon his ambition of taking Jerusalem. For the next year, skirmishing continued. Then, in September 1192, Saladin agreed to a three-year truce, which left Acre and a thin coastal strip in the hands of the crusaders. Christians were once more able to visit the holy places in Jerusalem.

As Richard headed home his ship was wrecked near Venice. He continued to travel overland, in disguise, but he was captured near Vienna in December 1192. His personal enemy, Leopold V of Austria, was the kidnapper. The English people then had to raise an enormous ransom of 150,000 marks. Its collection was organized by Eleanor of Aquitaine. Richard also had to surrender his kingdom, although it was returned to him as a fief.

When Richard had taken the throne, he had made John count of Mortain in southwest Normandy. In England John was given Peverel, Lancaster, Marlborough and Ludgershall – with their castles – along with Tickhill, Wallingford and the counties of Derby and Nottingham – without castles. Then Cornwall, Devon, Somerset, and Dorset were added on, giving him revenues of some £6,000 a year. John then married Isabella of Gloucester – in defiance of the archbishop of Canterbury's prohibition on the grounds of consanguinity – which gave him her father's estates. In March 1190, he was made heir to the duchy of Normandy. However, he had to promise that he would not enter England for three years while Richard was away on his crusade.

BELOW *Richard I made his reputation in the Third Crusade, but he failed to recapture Jerusalem from the Muslim leader Saladin.*

THE MAGNA CARTA

The Magna Carta, or Great Charter, was devised by the barons of King John, who wished to limit the powers of the monarch and make him govern according to feudal law. Civil war was threatening England in 1215, so King John appeased his nobles by signing the document at Runnymede in June 1215.

But the 63 clauses of the Magna Carta became much more than a political expedient. They lie at the heart of individual liberty in the United Kingdom, Ireland, the Commonwealth and the United States. Only three of the original 63 clauses are still in force in England but their importance cannot be overrated. For instance, the Petition of Right of 1628 and the *Habeas Corpus* Act of 1679 are closely based on clause 39, which states:

'No free man shall be taken or imprisoned, or be disseised [deprived] of his freehold, or liberties, or free customs, or be outlawed, or exiled, or any otherwise destroyed… except by lawful judgement of his peers, or by the law of the land.'

And in the United States, both the national and the state constitutions borrow from the Magna Carta. In fact, two of the clauses became the fifth and sixth amendments of the American Constitution.

Revisions to the document appeared at an early stage. The first of these was issued by the earl of Pembroke, regent of Henry III, in October 1216. Its purpose was to omit items that pertained to the political situation in 1215. The Magna Carta was again revised by Henry III's regent in November 1216, this time excluding the clauses that related to forests, which were transferred into a separate forestry charter. Then when Henry came of age in 1225 he felt the need to reissue the Magna Carta under his own seal. And Henry released another version in 1264, after his own conflict with the barons.

When Henry died in 1272, his son Edward I, or Edward Longshanks, sought to codify the law. He 'inspected' the Magna Carta and made it a part of his new statute rolls in 1297. By this time, it was down to just 37 clauses. These, the document said, were 'to be kept in our Kingdom of England forever'. Edward's version remained intact for over five centuries, but after that 34 clauses were repealed.

George IV opened the floodgates in 1829 when he repealed clause 26. Following that, 15 clauses were repealed by the Statute Law Revision Act of 1863 and the Statute Law (Ireland) Revision Act of 1872. Queen Victoria was responsible for the demise of another six clauses by the end of her reign. The lawmakers were hacking away at the Magna Carta as late as 1969, when six more clauses were removed. The three that remain are:

CLAUSE 1: First, We have granted to God, and by this our present Charter have confirmed, for Us and our Heirs for ever, that the Church of England shall be free, and shall have all her whole rights and liberties inviolable. We have granted also, and given to all the free men of our realm, for Us and Our heirs for ever, these liberties under-written, to have and to hold to them and their heirs, of Us and Our heirs for ever.
CLAUSE 13: The City of London shall have all the old liberties and customs. Furthermore We will and grant, that all other cities, boroughs, towns, and the barons of the five ports, and all other ports, shall have all their liberties and free customs.
CLAUSE 39: No free man shall be taken or imprisoned, or be disseised [deprived] of his freehold, or liberties, or free customs, or be outlawed, or exiled, or any otherwise destroyed; nor will We not pass upon him, nor condemn him, except by lawful judgement of his peers, or by the law of the land. We will sell to no man, we will not deny or defer to any man either justice or right.

ABOVE *King John was the villain that history has painted him. However, he was forced into signing the Magna Carta, the foundation of individual freedoms in England and all other Common-Law countries.*

But in October 1190, Richard named as his heir his three-year-old nephew Arthur, duke of Brittany, the son of his deceased brother Geoffrey. The news caused John to immediately break his promise – he landed in England and forced Richard's chancellor to flee to France. Looking to his own advantage, Philip II of France then attacked Richard's French territories on John's behalf.

Hoping to gain the throne, John spread the word that Richard was dead. But the lie did not convince the English people. John's castles were besieged and preparations were made to defend England against an invasion from France. When the ransom demand came from Austria, John realized that the game was up. Soon afterwards he received a message from Philip which said, 'The Devil is loosed'. Fearing that Richard

was about to be released and that he would soon be facing a charge of treason, John fled to France. Philip and John then offered to pay Richard's captors 80,000 marks if they would keep him out of harm's way.

When Richard was ransomed in 1194, he returned to England for a second coronation. Then John was banished and stripped of all his possessions. Within a month Richard was back in Normandy, having left England in the hands of Hubert Walter, his chief minister, and the archbishop of Canterbury.

However, by the following year John and Richard had become reconciled and some lands, including Mortain and Ireland, were returned to John. When Philip II captured Arthur of Brittany in 1196 Richard named his brother John as his heir.

The final years of Richard's life were spent fighting Philip II in an attempt to hold on to England's possessions in France. As well as fighting across Anjou, Maine, Touraine, Aquitaine and Gascony, Richard built major fortifications – including the great fort at Château-Gaillard, which stands above the village of Les Andelys. In 1199, while besieging the castle at Châlus, Richard was hit in the shoulder by an arrow from a crossbow. Gangrene set in and he died on 6 April, aged 42. Richard was buried in the abbey church at Fontevrault, beside his parents Henry II and Eleanor of Aquitaine.

BELOW Returning from the Crusades, Richard I was imprisoned in Austria. A lion was put in his cell to kill him. Instead, he killed it.

The Field at Runnymede

On Richard's death, John (r.1199–1216) was invested as duke of Normandy and crowned king of England. But Arthur, backed by Philip II, was recognized as Richard's successor in Maine and Anjou. In the following year, Philip II recognized John as the successor to all of Richard's French possessions, in return for money and territorial concessions.

John had his marriage to Isabella of Gloucester annulled and instead married Isabella of Angoulême. She had been betrothed to Hugh X de Lusignan, but John snatched her away for his own. The Lusignans rebelled, Philip II intervened and war broke out. In 1202 John took the opportunity to capture Arthur of Brittany at Mirebeau-en-Poitou. Arthur was imprisoned and according to tradition John caused him to be murdered. But after that, Normandy, Maine and Anjou were quickly lost to Philip.

John now spent most of his time in England. In order to pay for the war with France he raised taxes – imposing a special tax on Jews – and enforced feudal prerogatives. Pope Innocent III (in office 1198–1216) then rejected the latest archbishop of Canterbury, who had been nominated by John. During the ensuing hostilities the king was excommunicated. John had this punishment removed by paying a tribute of 1,000 marks. However, he had succeeded in alienating England's churchmen, along with the barons. There was an unsuccessful plot to murder him during a campaign against the Welsh.

John launched a final campaign in France in 1214, but he was forced to accept a truce. When he returned to England, the country was on the verge of rebellion. Despite lengthy negotiations, civil war broke out in the following year. When London turned against him John was forced to come to terms. On 15 June 1215, he met with his barons in a field at Runnymede. They brought with them a document containing their demands, known as the Articles of the Barons. After revisions were made, the king and the barons accepted what became known as the Magna Carta.

However, John had no intention of living up to the provisions of the document. He immediately wrote to Pope Innocent III asking him to annul the charter. Innocent complied by excommunicating the barons. Civil war broke out again, in the form of the First Barons' War. The barons called for help from the French Prince Louis – later Louis VIII (r.1223–6). Louis invaded England in 1216 and came perilously close to becoming king. John fought on until he died in the same year, leaving the problem to be resolved by the future Henry III.

BELOW *The coronation of Henry III. In government he displayed such an indifference to tradition that the barons forced on him a series of major reforms.*

ABOVE *At the Battle of Evesham in 1265, the royalist force defeated Simon de Montfort, ending the Second Barons' War.*

The Second Barons' War

Henry III was the first Planagenet to be born in England and to spend most of his life there. He was only nine years old when he was crowned, so the country was at first ruled by a series of regents. Henry took over when his minority ended. The rebel barons were defeated and Prince Louis was expelled. He was not a good administrator: an empty treasury did not prevent him from pursuing a series of costly foreign wars.

The problems began as early as 1237, when the barons objected to the influence of Henry's foreign relatives. Things got worse in the following year, when a marriage was arranged between his French-born favourite Simon de Montfort and his sister Eleanor, who had previously taken a vow of chastity. Then in 1242 Henry's Lusignan half-brothers involved him in a disastrously expensive military venture in France. The barons demanded a say in the selection of the king's counsellors, but Henry repeatedly rejected their proposals.

Henry's troubles did not end there. In 1254 he agreed to finance a papal war in Sicily on condition that Pope Innocent IV (in office 1243–54) put his infant son Edmund on the throne. Four years later Pope Alexander IV (in office 1254–61) threatened to excommunicate Henry for not paying up. Henry appealed to the barons, but they only agreed to help if he acceded to their demands. They got their way. In 1258, under the Provisions of Oxford, they created and selected a 15-member Privy Council. Its function was to advise the king and oversee the entire administration.

By this time, Simon de Montfort had become convinced that Henry was unfit to rule. Richard de Clare, earl of Gloucester, sided with Henry. When the king lent his support to Gloucester, civil war broke out. In May 1264 Simon de Montfort won a resounding victory at Lewes, capturing Henry and his eldest son Edward. De Montfort established a military dictatorship, ruling in Henry's name, but he did not have the support of the barons. Striving to find some way of instituting government by consent, he called a parliament – from the French *parlement,* meaning speaking. Composed of representatives of the boroughs and the shires, it formed the basis of the modern British Parliament.

In May 1265, Prince Edward escaped captivity and rallied the royalist forces. They defeated and killed de Montfort at the battle of Evesham in August of that year. By this time Henry was weak and senile. Edward took charge of the Government, before ruling in his own right as Edward I.

Edward Longshanks

Edward I (r.1272–1307), also known as Edward Longshanks, was also a crusader. He was in Sicily, on his way back from the Eighth Crusade, when he heard of

BELOW *Edward I – also known as Edward Longshanks – subdued the Welsh and developed Common Law, which England later bestowed on much of the world.*

his father's death. After his coronation in 1272, he was determined to enforce his primacy in the British Isles, starting with Wales. He invaded Wales in 1277, defeated the Welsh leader, Llywelyn ap Gruffydd, and then built a ring of castles to enforce his authority. When his rule provoked rebellion, he invaded again. Gruffydd was killed in battle in 1282 and his brother Dafydd was executed for 'treason', ending Welsh hopes of independence. Wales was then brought into the English legal and administrative framework. In 1301 Edward's son was proclaimed Prince of Wales – all male heirs to the English throne have adopted the title ever since.

Edward was responsible for a variety of legal and administrative reforms. For instance, he asserted the rights of the crown, promoted the uniform administration of justice and codified the legal system. He also pursued a series of costly military campaigns that required increases in taxation. This in turn led to Parliament meeting more regularly until, by the end of his reign, the parliamentary process had become an established feature of political life.

The king's need for money also led to the expulsion of the Jews from England. When Edward passed the 'Edict of Expulsion' in 1290, which formally expelled all Jews from England, he was able to confiscate all of the Jews' money and property.

Edward attempted to extend his rule to Scotland, but his diplomatic overtures forced the Scots into an alliance with the French. So he invaded and conquered the nation in 1296 – after which the Stone of Scone was removed and taken to

THE STONE OF SCONE

Also known as the Stone of Destiny, the Stone of Scone is said to have been the pillow on which Jacob beheld a vision of angels. It perhaps reached Ireland in about 700BC, after which it was set up on the Hill of Tara, where the kings of Ireland were crowned. After being seized by marauding Scots, it ended up in the village of Scone in about AD840. Until the 13th century, all of the kings of Scotland were seated on it during their coronation ceremonies.

Edward I removed the stone in 1296 and took it to Westminster Abbey. He had it fitted under a special throne called the Coronation Chair, so that all future kings of England could also be crowned king of Scotland. But that did not happen until James VI of Scotland was also crowned James I of England in 1603.

In 1950, the Stone was stolen by a group of Scottish nationalists, who took it back to Scotland. It was recovered and returned to Westminster Abbey four months later. However, in 1996, John Major's government finally returned the stone to Scotland.

RIGHT *The Stone of Scone used to reside in the Coronation Chair, where British monarchs were simultaneously crowned king, or queen, of England and Scotland.*

Westminster. Sir William Wallace led an uprising against Edward, but he was captured in 1305 before being executed for treason. In the following year the Scottish nobleman Robert the Bruce then rebelled. Edward was on his way to fight Bruce when he died near Carlisle on 7 July 1307. His tomb in Westminster Abbey bears the inscription, 'Here lies Edward the Hammer of the Scots'. He was succeeded by Edward II.

Ordinances of 1311

Born on 25 April 1284, Edward II (r. 1307–27) was the fourth son of Edward I of England. He became king by default because he was the only surviving brother out of the original four. Edward immediately recalled Piers Gaveston from exile – his favourite and probably his lover. Edward's father Edward I had banished Gaveston to France because he thought he was a bad influence on his son. Gaveston was given the earldom of Cornwall, a title that was normally only conferred on royalty. This was hugely unpopular with the barons, who demanded that he be

banished again. Edward was forced to give in and send Gaveston to Ireland, but he returned after only a year.

In 1311, a committee of 21 barons issued the 'Ordinances of 1311', which demanded Gaveston's banishment and attempted to limit the royal control of finances and appointments. Gaveston went to Flanders, but secretly returned. When Edward publicly restored him, the barons took up arms. But Edward deserted his favourite, and he was captured and killed.

Edward then attempted to emulate his father and subdue Scotland. But he was decisively defeated by Robert the Bruce at the Battle of Bannockburn in 1314. Not only that, but Edward's realm was now in the hands of the barons. They were headed by Edward's cousin, Thomas of Lancaster, who had made himself the effective ruler of England by 1315. However, Lancaster proved incompetent and parts of the country collapsed into anarchy.

By 1318, Edward and Lancaster had been partly reconciled, but the king had two new favourites – Hugh le Despenser and his son – who were again thought to be his lovers. When Edward supported the Despensers' ambitions in Wales, Lancaster banished them. But by removing the Despensers Lancaster had opened the door to a surge of nobles, all vying for Edward's favour. With their support Edward took up arms and defeated Lancaster at the Battle of Boroughbridge in March 1322. Lancaster was executed and Edward recalled the Despensers, who then ruled alongside him. This did not please Edward's queen, the famous beauty Isabella of France. While on a diplomatic mission to Paris in 1325, she became the mistress of Roger Mortimer. In September 1326, the couple invaded England – and there was virtually no resistance. The Despensers

LEFT *Isabella of France was a famous beauty, but her husband Edward II was more interested in male companions. Scorning his wife led to his downfall.*

ROBERT THE BRUCE

ABOVE *Robert the Bruce freed Scotland from English rule, defeating Edward II at the Battle of Bannockburn on 24 June 1314.*

On 11 July 1274 Robert the Bruce was born into an aristocratic Scottish family with roots in Scotland and Normandy. He was related by marriage to the Scottish royal family and his grandfather was one of the many claimants to the throne when it became vacant in 1290. Civil war was avoided when Edward I was called in to arbitrate. The English king decided that John Balliol had the strongest claim and he was duly crowned. But Balliol's weakness allowed Edward to dominate Scotland for some years. When Balliol finally challenged the English king in 1296 his army was annihilated. Edward and his overlords then ruled Scotland as a province of England.

Sir William Wallace led a campaign against the English, supported by Bruce and the Comyn family, but he was defeated at Falkirk in 1298. However, Scottish opposition to the English continued, led by Bruce and the Comyns. Edward's army carried on attacking the Scottish garrisons until 1305, when Wallace's execution appeared to signal the end of Scottish resistance.

But the situation suddenly changed in 1306. A church in Dumfries was the scene of a meeting between Bruce and his rival for the throne, John Comyn, Balliol's nephew. A quarrel developed and Bruce fatally wounded Comyn. Bruce was outlawed by Edward and excommunicated by the pope, but he could now proclaim himself king. He was crowned Robert I (r.1306–29) at Scone on 27 March 1306. In the following year, Bruce was deposed by Edward's army and forced to flee. He spent the winter on an island off the coast of Antrim but his wife and daughters were imprisoned and three of his brothers were executed.

On his return to Scotland, Bruce waged a guerrilla war against the English, now ruled by Edward II. At the Battle of Bannockburn in June 1314 he defeated a much larger English army, paving the way to an independent Scottish monarchy. Two years later, Robert's brother Edward was inaugurated as high king of Ireland, but he was killed in battle in 1318. In that same year Robert the Bruce captured Berwick but Edward II still refused to give up his claim to Scotland. Finally, in 1320, the Scottish nobles sent a letter to the pope. The 'Declaration of Arbroath' asserted the antiquity of the Scottish people and their monarchy and declared that Robert the Bruce should be Scotland's rightful king. He received papal confirmation four years later.

When Edward II was deposed in favour of Edward III, the English made peace with Scotland. The Treaty of Northampton was signed in 1328, in which England renounced all of its claims to Scotland and recognized Robert I as king. He died only a year later, on 7 June 1329. Although he was buried at Dunfermline he had requested that his heart be taken to the Holy Land. However, it only got as far as Spain. It was then returned to Scotland and was buried in Melrose Abbey.

were captured and executed and Edward was deposed. The son of Edward and Isabella, the future Edward III, was chosen to rule and he was crowned in January 1327.

Edward II was imprisoned at Berkeley Castle in Gloucestershire. He was later found dead in his cell. There was no evidence of poison nor any sign of a stab wound on his body. The rumour soon circulated that if the corpse were to be intimately examined, burn marks would be found in 'those parts in which he had been wont to take his vicious pleasure'. It was said that a red-hot poker had been forced up his rectum.

The Long War Begins

Edward III (r.1327–77) was 14 years old when he came to the throne. His mother and her lover, Roger Mortimer, ruled in Edward's name until 1330. The 18-year-old Edward then took his revenge – Mortimer was executed and his mother was exiled to Castle Rising. By then, Edward had married Philippa of Hainault who gave him fourteen children.

As ever, there were ongoing territorial disputes with France. This time the argument was about English rule in Gascony and control of the Bordeaux-based wine trade. The new French king Philip VI (r.1328–50) then allied himself with Scotland and sought to retaliate by disrupting the English wool trade in Flanders. In 1337, Edward revived his claim to the crown of France, beginning a conflict that dragged on for a century. The Hundred Years' War, as it was called, resolved nothing, however. It was not until 1801 that George III dropped England's claim to the French crown.

In 1340, Edward personally led the English fleet in a great sea battle off the Flemish city of Sluis – the French navy was practically destroyed. But when the fighting became land-based the English

treasury ran out of funds. Edward was forced to make a truce, after which he returned to England and rebuilt Windsor Castle.

In July 1346 Edward broke the truce and landed in Normandy, accompanied by his son Edward, the Black Prince. His decisive victory at Crécy in August scattered the French army and demonstrated the superiority of the English longbow over the armoured knights of the French. Edward then captured Calais after a 12-month siege. He ejected the French inhabitants and colonized it with Englishmen in order to establish it as a base for future campaigns. The English won further victories in Gascony and Brittany but a lack of funds was again the cause of a premature English withdrawal.

While Edward was in France, Philip VI persuaded his ally David II of Scotland (r.1329–71) to invade England on his behalf. But the Scots were routed at Neville's Cross near Durham and King David was captured. When the king returned to England in 1348 he created the Order of the Garter, Britain's highest civil and military honour. In the same year bubonic plague, known as the Black Death, made its first appearance in England. It is thought that at least half of the population succumbed to the disease. Among other things, it was now more difficult to assemble an efficient army.

The war with the French resumed in 1355. In the following year, the Black Prince won a significant victory at Poitiers, capturing the French king

ABOVE *Edward III led England into the Hundred Years' War. His descendants fought over the throne, resulting in the Wars of the Roses.*

ABOVE *Queen Philippa pleads with her husband, Edward III, for the lives of the Burghers of Calais after the siege of the city.*

left the fighting to his sons. They enjoyed little success and the English lost much of the territory they had gained in 1360.

After the death of his queen, Philippa of Hainault in 1369, Edward fell under the influence of his mistress Alice Perrers, on whom he lavished gifts – including land. Then against a backdrop of military failure in France and the outbreak of the plague, the 'Good Parliament' of 1376 was summoned. Its members resolved to clean up the corrupt royal council. Alice Perrers and other members of the court were impeached for profiting out of the royal finances and new councillors were imposed on the king. It was during Edward's reign that Parliament was first split into two chambers.

While the Good Parliament was sitting Edward the Black Prince, the king's heir, died. So when Edward III died on 21 June 1377, his grandson, the Black Prince's son, succeeded as Richard II.

The Fall of Richard II

Born in Bordeaux on 6 January 1367, Richard II (r.1377–99) became king at the age of ten. But his uncle, John of Gaunt, the duke of Lancaster, held the reins of power at that time. He had also ruled in Edward's stead during his frequent absences in France. John of Gaunt was extremely unpopular with the people, not least because conditions were harsh in that period. The Black Death had left the country with a shortage of labour, so wages and prices had soared. Parliament passed legislation to restrain wages, but prices were left unregulated. Then a poll tax was introduced. All of this came to a head as the Peasants' Revolt of 1381. Richard, still a boy, bravely rode out to meet the rebels, who were led by Wat Tyler. The king agreed to the rebels' demands, but he would later go back on his word. Tyler was killed and

John II (r.1350–64), also known as John the Good. The resulting Treaty of Brétigny in 1360 marked the end of the first phase of the Hundred Years' War and was the high point of English influence in France. The treaty ceded much of southwest France to England and fixed John II's ransom at three million gold écus. John was released so that he could raise the ransom, but his place had to be taken by hostages. When one of them – John's own son – escaped, John felt dishonoured. He returned to England to surrender himself.

In 1369, the French declared war again. Edward, by now an elderly man,

THE HUNDRED YEARS' WAR

At first the Hundred Years' War went well for the English, with victories at Sluis (1340), Crécy (1346) and Poitiers (1356). The Treaty of Brétigny (1360) confirmed the recovery of Aquitaine. However, with the death of the Black Prince in 1376, and the accession of Richard II, the English went on the defensive. After 1380, both England and France were preoccupied with internal power struggles. Henry V renewed the assault, winning a famous battle at Agincourt in 1415. By 1422, the English and their Burgundian allies controlled Aquitaine and all of France north of the Loire, including Paris.

According to the Treaty of Troyes, signed on 21 May 1420, Henry V was recognized as heir and regent to Charles VI of France (r.1380–1422). Henry sealed the deal by marrying Charles' daughter Catherine on 2 June. But Henry died of camp fever on 31 August 1422 and Charles VI died on 21 October, so the French throne passed to the Dauphin. Athough he was crowned Charles VII, France remained under the regency of the duke of Bedford.

Henry V left his nine-month-old son Henry VI on the throne, but from 1428 Joan of Arc began to turn the tide against the English. By 1453 Calais was the only remaining English possession in France.

LEFT *A copper-plate engraving showing the Battle of Agincourt, fought on 25 October 1415. Henry V's death a few years later prevented him taking the French throne and ending the Hundred Years' War.*

ABOVE *Joan of Arc rallied the French to fight against the English. Although the Hundred Years' War continued for another 22 years after her death, she helped secure victory.*

ROBERT THE BRUCE

The Black Death, which lasted from about 1348 to 1350, had disrupted the social and economic fabric of England. The shortage of labour meant that the peasants could now demand better rewards — even freedom, from their feudal obligations. But Edward III's Statute of Labourers, passed in 1351, severely restricted wages and removed the right of workers to change employers.

On top of that a poll tax had been introduced as a way of financing the wars in France. It started at four pence a head in 1377 but by 1381 the charge had trebled to 12 pence. The revolt began with attacks on tax collectors but then it became more widespread. Peasants attacked their feudal masters and destroyed the documents that condemned them to the status of villeins — or serfs. The lawyers who wrote these documents were also attacked, as were the religious houses that upheld the feudal system.

There was a general uprising across southeast England. The men of Essex and Kent marched on London. Admitted to the city by

ABOVE *Wat Tyler, leader of the Peasants' Revolt, is killed by Sir William Walworth, supposedly for insolence, in the presence of Richard II.*

sympathizers, they attacked Fleet Prison and John of Gaunt's Savoy Palace. At that point the 14-year-old Richard II rode out to meet the protesters at Mile End. After hearing their grievances he made a series of promises. But later that day other protesters broke into the Tower of London, then the seat of government, and executed all of the officials, including the lord chancellor and the lord treasurer.

On the following day the king met the rebels again, this time at Smithfield. During the negotiations that took place the peasants' leader, Wat Tyler, was attacked and killed by the mayor of London. His followers had exhausted their supplies, so they drifted home. Richard II then went back on all the promises he had made, declaring 'Villeins ye are and villeins ye shall remain'. It is thought that this early victory gave the king an exalted sense of his own power.

LEFT *Pestdoctors in masks and gowns tried to prevent the spread of the Black Death when it hit England in 1347. But at that time, no one knew what caused the pestilence.*

the authorities quickly regained control.

When Richard II became old enough to rule in his own right, many resented the small group of favourites that surrounded him. So his request for the means to pursue his French wars gave Parliament the chance to demand their dismissal. Richard refused, provoking them to impeach his chancellor, the earl of Suffolk. They also created a commission to oversee Richard's activities. The king tried to retaliate but in 1388 a group of his leading opponents, the 'Lords Appellant', brought an appeal of treason against his closest allies. They suffered various fates, some being executed.

Richard had been humiliated, but he complied with the appellants' demands. He made a truce with France before cutting taxes and then spent eight years working in apparent harmony with his critics. In the meantime, he created a quasi-religious dimension of kingship. He introduced new forms of address, demanding to be called 'Your Highness' or 'Your Majesty' rather than 'My Lord'. Then he staged 'crown-wearings' in Westminster Abbey and travelled to Ireland to receive the homage of the local chieftains, or 'high kings'.

Two years later he sought to impose this same exalted vision of kingship on England. In 1397 he arrested and tried three of the Lords Appellant. Gloucester and Arundel were imprisoned and executed, Warwick was banished to the Isle of Man. The king was granted revenues for life and the powers of Parliament were delegated to a committee.

In September 1398, a quarrel between two former appellants, John of Gaunt's son Henry Bolingbroke and Thomas Mowbray, duke of Norfolk, gave the king the opportunity to banish them both. When John of Gaunt died in February 1399 Richard confiscated his vast Lancastrian estates, which would have passed to Bolingbroke. In May, his coffers now full, Richard left to campaign in Ireland. Bolingbroke seized the opportunity to invade England, rallying both noble and popular support.

When Richard returned to England in August he surrendered without a fight. He had abdicated by September, allowing Bolingbroke to ascend the throne as Henry IV (r.1399–1413). In October Richard was imprisoned in Pontefract Castle, where he was executed four months later, the first victim of the Wars of the Roses. His body was buried for a time in King's Langley, Hertfordshire. However, in the reign of Henry V, Richard's remains were placed in the tomb he had built for himself in Westminster Abbey.

BELOW *Richard II appeases the rebels after the death of Wat Tyler, defusing the Peasants' Revolt and preserving the power of the crown.*

IRELAND

RIGHT *An engraving showing William III at the Battle of the Boyne, where his forces were successful in suppressing the Glorious Revolution.*

A number of Anglo-Norman adventurers had conquered most of the eastern part of Ireland before Henry II arrived there in October 1171. He granted them rights to the lands they had taken, while keeping the major cities for himself. The remaining Irish rulers, except those in the northwest, were forced to recognize Henry's supremacy. Other Normans established themselves in Ulster but the high king of Ireland, Roderic O'Connor, was demoted to king of Connaught, although he was still charged with collecting tribute from the other kings. He became so unpopular with his own people that he was forced to abdicate.

When King John visited Ireland in 1210, he set up a central government that was independent of the feudal lords. An Irish exchequer had been established in 1200, and a chancery followed in 1232. For administrative purposes, the country was divided into counties. English law was introduced and an attempt was made to limit the feudal liberties of the Anglo-Norman barons. A parliament was set up along the lines of the one in England but only the Anglo-Irish were represented. Native Irishmen were excluded.

Edward Bruce, brother of Robert the Bruce, tried to wrest Ireland from the English, but he was killed in battle at Faughart near Dundalk in 1318. English control was strengthened by the introduction of new earldoms. After that, the native Celts reasserted themselves politically and the Anglo-Irish pursued integration by marrying Irish women and adopting Gaelic customs. However, Edward III's son, Lionel, duke of Clarence, who was governor from 1361 until 1367, attempted to separate the two cultures. He delineated the English-controlled lands, known as the Pale, and then outlawed intermarriage by means of the Statute of Kilkenny.

During the Wars of the Roses Ireland supported the Yorkists, but Edward IV found the country no easier to control than others had before him. In 1468, Edward ordered the execution of the earl of Desmond. This enabled the earls of Kildare to take on the role of viceroy. But after he supported Lambert Simnel and Perkin Warbeck, the pretenders to the English throne, the eighth earl of Kildare, the Great Earl, was removed from the post. Fearing a rebellion, Henry VII sent Sir Edward Poynings to restore order. Poynings met with some success but he could not fill Kildare's shoes, so Henry VII restored Kildare. However, a later earl of Kildare, the tenth earl, saw fit to renounce his allegiance to Henry VIII and was executed in 1537. There would be no more Irish-born viceroys for more than a century.

The enmity between the Irish and the English increased with the Reformation and Henry's confiscation of monastic lands. Even the Anglo-Irish refused to break their ties with the pope. However it was the Catholic Queen Mary who organized the colonization of Irish lands by Englishmen – the plantations. When the Protestant Church was established by Elizabeth I, the Irish were only required to pay lip service. Nevertheless they rose up in protest and a series of rebellions broke out. One of these, the Desmond rebellion, was a papally backed crusade against Elizabeth. It ended with the slaughter of the rebels and their Italian and Spanish allies. On top of all that, it allowed the English to confiscate a large area of Munster, which became a further plantation. A second revolt – the Tyrone Rebellion – again backed by the Spanish, met with similar disaster.

Ireland then became embroiled in the English Civil War. The victory of the Puritans was understandably ill-received by the Irish Catholics. Oliver Cromwell afterwards subdued the country during a brutal campaign that remains controversial to this day. In 1653 the last of the organized Irish armies surrendered and Irish representatives began attending Parliament in London.

After James II, a declared Catholic, was deposed in the Glorious Revolution, he raised an army in Ireland. It was defeated at the Battle of the Boyne in 1690 by William III of England (William of Orange). This resulted in the forfeiture of large tracts of land owned by James' supporters, so reducing Catholic landownership. By 1703, Catholics owned less than 15 per cent of the land in Ireland.

The Test Act of 1704 bolstered the Protestant position even further. It stated that only those who received communion in the Church of Ireland could hold office. Consequently, all political power was in the hands of the ten per cent of Irish who were Protestant. Accordingly, Ireland's parliament began to lose power to its English counterpart. Alarmed by the American War of Independence and the French Revolution, the British government sought to secure the loyalty of Catholics by extending suffrage to them. Nevertheless, Protestants and Catholics united under the Irish revolutionary Wolf Tone in 1791 – their rebellion was again unsuccessful. Finally, the British under William Pitt decided that the only solution was to end Irish independence. So in 1801 the United Kingdom of Great Britain and Ireland was formed. There would be a single parliament in London, in which the Irish would have 100 members.

However, the Catholic majority in Ireland remained economically disadvantaged and scarcely benefited from the Industrial Revolution that was enriching the rest of the nation. When a potato blight from America hit Ireland in 1840, the Government far away in London was slow to react. A million people died of starvation and many emigrated – so many that the population halved. Out of all this sprang the failed Home Rule movement. The Irish then took up arms, which won independence for the south in 1920.

ABOVE *Wolfe Tone sought to overthrow English rule in Ireland, bringing a French military force to support the insurrection that broke out in 1798.*

CHAPTER FOUR
IV

THE HOUSES OF LANCASTER AND YORK

THE HOUSES OF LANCASTER AND YORK

Henry IV (1399–1413)

Henry V (1413–22)

Henry VI (1422–61, 1470–1)

Edward IV (1461–70, 1471–83)

Edward V (1483)

Richard III (1483–5)

Dates show reign of monarch

LEFT *George Plantagenet, duke of Clarence, conspired against his brother, Edward IV, during the Wars of the Roses. Rumour had it that he was drowned in a butt of Malmsey wine.*

ABOVE *Archbishop of Canterbury Thomas Arundel preached in favour of Bolingbroke, the duke of Lancaster, who deposed Richard II and made himself Edward IV.*

The First Lancastrian King

Henry IV (r.1399–1413) was born at Bolingbroke Castle in Lincolnshire in April 1366. His father was John of Gaunt, duke of Lancaster, the third surviving son of Edward III and the uncle of Richard II. His mother Blanche was descended from Henry III.

When Richard II became king in 1377 Henry became a member of the opposition leaders, the Lords Appellant. He was banished after an argument with another member of the court in 1398. It was the last straw when he was deprived of his inheritance, following John of Gaunt's death. Henry invaded England in 1399 and was crowned king in October of the same year, after asserting that Richard had abdicated of his own free will. Thus Henry Bolingbroke became the first king of the Lancastrian line.

Richard's half-brothers immediately rose on his behalf, but they were put down. In 1400 Richard's body had to be put on display in London in order to dispel the rumour that he was still alive. Later that year, the Welsh squire Owain Glyndwr raised a national rebellion against English rule. In 1403, Glyndwr allied himself with one of King Henry's opponents, the powerful Henry Percy, earl of Northumberland, and his son

OWAIN GLYNDWR AND THE WELSH UPRISING

Owain Glyndwr (Owen Glendower), a descendant of the princes of Powys and heir to several manors in north Wales, was born in around 1354. He was educated in England, after which he joined the English army and took part in an invasion of Scotland. When he returned to Wales in 1399, he found that Richard II's oppressive rule had ruined the economy and stirred up popular resentment. But Richard's time was almost over because Henry Bolingbroke usurped the throne shortly afterwards.

In September 1400 Glyndwr's long-running land dispute with his neighbour, Reynold, Lord Grey of Ruthin, escalated into an uprising. The conflict quickly turned into a struggle for Welsh independence.

Glyndwr formed an alliance with Henry IV's powerful opponent, the earl of Northumberland. First of all, the Welsh captured Conwy Castle in April 1401. Then, in June 1402, at the Battle of Pilleth on Bryn Glas Hill, Glyndwr led his troops to victory over an English army led by

ABOVE *Owain Glyndwr proclaimed himself prince of Wales in the last major attempt by the Welsh to throw off English rule.*

Edmund Mortimer. By 1404, he controlled most of Wales. He set up a Welsh parliament, styled himself prince of Wales and began governing his newly independent state.

However, in 1405 Prince Henry – later Henry V – defeated him twice. His allies in England were also routed and support for the rebellion faded. In the same year a French expeditionary force landed at Milford Haven, before joining the Welsh in a march on Worcester. They captured several important castles as they went, but it was too late – the English had already started to regain control of Wales. By 1409 Prince Henry had captured Glyndwr's main stronghold. Glyndwr continued a guerrilla war until 1412, but nothing more was heard of him. In February 1416 terms were offered for his surrender, but it is thought that he was probably dead by then.

BELOW *Henry V crushed all resistance in England before heading for France where he sought to claim the throne.*

Henry, better known as Hotspur. Hotspur's brief uprising, the most serious challenge Henry faced, ended when he was killed in battle near Shrewsbury in July 1403. In the aftermath, a number of nobles, including the archbishop of York, were executed for treason. Northumberland's subsequent rebellion in 1408 was quickly suppressed. It was

the last armed challenge to Henry's authority. By this time Henry was suffering from what contemporaries called leprosy, but it might have been congenital syphilis.

Henry made a number of fruitless expeditions to Wales, but his son Prince Henry – later Henry V (r.1413–22) – had broken the back of the rebellion by 1409. The king also had to fight off Scottish border raids and the French, who sided with the Welsh. In order to finance these activities, he was forced to rely on parliamentary grants. From 1401 to 1406 Parliament repeatedly accused him of financial mismanagement. The Government was gradually gaining control over royal expenditure and appointments.

As Henry's health deteriorated, a power struggle developed between his favourite, Thomas Arundel, archbishop of Canterbury, and Prince Henry. Then in 1411 Arundel was ousted. There were also disagreements between father and son. Prince Henry wanted to resume war in France, where a civil war had broken out, but the king favoured peace. Uneasy relations between the prince and his father persisted until Henry IV's death in London on 20 March 1413.

The Victor of Agincourt

Prince Henry then became Henry V (r.1413–22) on 9 April 1413. His only challenge came in 1415 when there was a conspiracy to put Edmund Mortimer, earl of March, on the throne. Some saw Mortimer as the rightful heir to the childless Richard II because he was the great-grandson of Lionel, duke of Clarence, the second surviving son of Edward III. But Henry

THE LOLLARDS

The Lollards were the precursors of the 16th-century Protestant Reformation. Their name comes from the Middle Dutch *lollaerd,* or 'mumbler' – a pejorative term for a heretic. They were followers of the 14th-century Oxford theologian John Wycliffe, who believed that the Church was too worldly and that the papacy had no justification in Scripture. He was charged with heresy, but never brought to trial. At his instigation, the Bible was translated into English, which an order of Poor Preachers then took to the people.

Wycliffe's followers in Oxford formed the first group of Lollards, but his ideas soon found a wider following because of the anticlerical sentiments stirred up by the Peasants' Revolt. But Henry IV began to repress heresy when he came to the throne. In 1401 came the first English statute that authorized the burning of heretics. The unfortunate William Sawtrey was actually burned a few days before the statute became law, thereby becoming the first Lollard martyr.

A Lollard uprising was crushed by Henry V in 1414. The movement then went underground, only to surface again in the 1500s, when Protestantism came to England.

RIGHT *Radical theologian John Wycliffe was a forerunner of the Protestant Reformation, but he escaped the persecution for heresy that many of his followers suffered.*

crushed the rebellion and Mortimer himself remained loyal to Henry, even fighting alongside him in France. Mortimer died of the plague while serving as the lieutenant of Ireland in 1423. Being childless, his claim to the throne passed to his nephew Richard, duke of York.

Henry then turned his attention to France in order to distract the English from their internal rivalries. This was a popular move because the nobles were eager for the spoils of war. Parliament willingly voted money for the campaign and Henry retained the support of the Church by persecuting the dissenting Lollards, who had previously been encouraged by John of Gaunt.

The king sailed for France, capturing the port of Harfleur. Then on 25 October 1415 he routed the French at the Battle of Agincourt. Between 1417

ABOVE *Henry VI came to the throne at the age of nine months. His uncles and cousins continued the wars in France in his name. Later his wife conspired against him.*

OPPOSITE *Joan of Arc kneels before Charles VII. Her victories against the English led to Charles being crowned king of France in Reims.*

The Loss of France

Henry VI (r.1422–61 and 1470–1) was born at Windsor Castle on 6 December 1421. Although he succeeded his father straight away, he was not crowned king of England until 1429. Two years after that, in 1431, he was crowned king of France in Paris. However, both England and France were ruled by regents during Henry's minority.

Henry was little interested in government. Instead he was very pious, concerned only with religious observance and education. As a result, his court was torn apart by rivalries between powerful ministers.

In France, the successes of the Dauphin and Joan of Arc began to weaken England's grip. Joan of Arc was born at Domrémy in France on around 6 January 1412. She first became conscious of her 'voices' in 1425. According to her testimony the voices were those of the saints, who were urging her to lead France to military victory. Her obvious conviction won her an audience with the Dauphin, later Charles VII. After gaining the approval of the Church scholars at Poitiers, she was then granted titular command of the French army. Under her leadership the siege of Orléans was lifted on 8 May 1429 and the English army was defeated at Patay on 18 June.

After accepting the surrender of the city of Troyes, Joan's army escorted Charles to Rheims for his coronation on 17 July. She made an unsuccessful attack on Paris on 8 September, but captured Saint-Pierre-le-Moutier on 4 November. As a reward for her service, Charles VII raised her to the nobility on 29 December 1429. Despite predicting her own defeat she returned to the field in the following year.

Captured at Compiègne by England's Burgundian allies on 23 May 1430, Joan

and 1419 Henry completed the conquest of Normandy. Rouen surrendered in January 1419 and he forced the French king to sign the Treaty of Troyes in May 1420. This recognized Henry as regent and heir to the throne of France. He strengthened his position even further by marrying Catherine of Valois, the king's daughter, in June. In February 1421 Henry was at last able to return to England with Catherine. It would be his first visit in three and a half years. The couple made a royal progress around the country. He returned to France in June 1422, but on 31 August of the same year he died suddenly of camp fever. His nine-month-old son would succeed him.

was handed over to the English. Her trial in Rouen appears to have been unfair and inconsistent in the extreme. In the end, many of the examining clergy had to be coerced into finding her guilty. Convicted as a heretic, she was burnt at the stake on 30 May 1431.

In an attempt to gain a period of peace with France, Henry VI signed the Treaty of Tours in 1444. According to the terms of the treaty, there would be a truce between England and France if certain conditions were met. One of them was Henry's marriage to Margaret of Anjou. But the fighting resumed. Normandy was lost in 1450 and by 1453 only Calais was left in English hands.

The Yorkists and the Lancastrians

Henry VI had a mental breakdown in July 1453 and Richard, duke of York, was made Protector. York had a better claim to the throne than Henry through Edward III's third and fifth sons –
Lionel, duke of Clarence and Edmund, duke of York.

The king recovered in 1455, at which point York raised an army. Henry was captured at St Albans. So began the civil war known as the Wars of the Roses. When Henry had a further breakdown, York resumed the regency (1455–6). In order to maintain peace, Henry was forced to recognize him as heir to the throne. It was left to Henry's queen, Margaret of Anjou, to organize the Lancastrian resistance.

BELOW *Margaret of Anjou was the consort of Henry VI who led the Lancastrians during the Wars of the Roses in the hope of putting her son Prince Edward on the throne.*

THE WARS OF THE ROSES

Also known as the 'Cousins' War', the Wars of the Roses were a series of wars between the Lancastrian and the Yorkist descendants of Edward III. The wars were so named because each of the houses had a rose for its symbol – red for Lancaster and white for York.

Edward's seven sons and five daughters ensured that there would be no shortage of claimants to the throne in the years following his death. It is often said that the Wars of the Roses started in 1455 with the First Battle of St Albans. However, the antagonism between the houses of Lancaster and York began in 1399 when Henry IV, the son of John of Gaunt, duke of Lancaster, usurped the throne from the last Angevin king, Richard II. Then in 1461 it was the turn of the Yorkists when Edward IV, son of Richard, duke of York, deposed Henry VI.

The Wars of the Roses finally came to an end when Richard III, a Yorkist monarch, was dethroned by Henry Tudor in 1485. Henry's claim to the throne was through his mother, Margaret Beaufort, who was descended from a son of John of Gaunt. The final act of reconciliation came when Henry Tudor, as Henry VII, married Elizabeth of York.

ABOVE *Elizabeth of York, sister of the Princes in the Tower (see page 89), and mother of Henry VIII.*

Richard, duke of York was killed at the Battle of Wakefield in December 1460, together with his chief supporter, the powerful Richard Neville. York's son Edward took over the Yorkist cause, while Neville's son became the new earl of Warwick – known to history as 'Warwick the Kingmaker'. The new duke of York, born in Rouen, was crowned Edward IV (r.1461–70 and 1471–83) in London on 4 March 1461. Henry was deposed, imprisoned in the Tower of London and then exiled to Scotland.

With the support of the earl of Warwick, Edward then defeated the Lancastrians in a series of battles, culminating in the Battle of Towton in 1461.

Warwick had hoped to arrange Edward's marriage to a suitable French noblewoman in order to strengthen England's position in France. However, to his dismay, the king had secretly married Elizabeth Woodville in May 1464. Edward had also rewarded his wife's relatives with high positions. Warwick then turned against him, choosing instead

ABOVE *Richard Neville, the earl of Warwick, was killed at the Battle of Barnet in 1471. He was known as 'the Kingmaker', obtaining the crown for the Yorkist Edward IV and restoring the deposed Lancastrian Henry VI.*

to ally himself with Edward's brother George, duke of Clarence. In August 1469, Warwick and Clarence seized and briefly detained Edward and his wife. They went on to execute her father and one of her brothers.

Edward then had to put down a rebellion in the north that had been engineered by Warwick. After the king had managed to quell the rebels Warwick and Clarence fled to France, where Warwick allied himself with Margaret of Anjou. Supported by Margaret's Lancastrian army, Warwick returned to England in September 1470 and drove Edward IV into exile in the Netherlands. He then put Henry VI back on the throne.

But Edward was not finished yet. He landed in the north in March 1471 and was restored to kingship in April. In the same month, Warwick was killed at the Battle of Barnet while Margaret's forces were destroyed at Tewkesbury in May. Edward, prince of Wales, Henry's son, also died in the battle. Henry VI died in the Tower soon afterwards. It is thought that he was murdered by Edward's brother Richard, duke of Gloucester – later Richard III (r.1483–5) – who is also credited with killing Henry's son, Prince Edward. Some people also suggested that Gloucester had a hand in the death of his elder brother, the rebellious George, duke of Clarence, who was executed in the Tower of London in 1478. The

ABOVE *Edward IV met Louis XI on the bridge at Picquigny. For a payment of 75,000 gold crowns down and 50,000 gold crowns a year, Edward agreed to withdraw from France.*

rumour circulated that Clarence had been drowned in a butt of Malmsey wine.

With his position strengthened, Edward IV was now eager to revive his claim to the French throne. In 1475 he headed for France, supported by a large grant from Parliament. It is said that he led the largest army that had ever left England. However, Louis XI avoided a fight by buying Edward off. The Treaty of Picquigny guaranteed Edward an immediate 75,000 gold crowns and an annuity of 50,000 gold crowns if he returned to England in peace. It was an offer he could not refuse. With that money, and the revenues from the Lancastrian estates he had confiscated, Edward lived in comfort for the rest of his life. Able to bear the cost of government himself, he had little need of Parliament. After establishing commercial treaties with France, Burgundy and the Hanseatic League – a confederation of the trading ports of the Baltic – he benefited from customs duties and trading in his own right.

Now independently wealthy, Edward reformed the administration and, in the name of his infant son, established a council to rule Wales. He was also a friend and patron of William Caxton, who brought printing to England. In 1757 Edward's royal library was given to the newly established British Museum by George II. It now forms part of the Royal Library, which is housed in the British Library.

Edward IV died suddenly on 9 April 1483, at the age of 40, leaving the crown to his 12-year-old son Edward.

ABOVE After taking Louis XI's money to drop his claim to the French throne, Edward IV lived comfortably without depending on grants from Parliament.

RIGHT Edward V was born while his father was briefly deposed and exiled in Holland. After taking the throne, he too was deposed and possibly murdered by his brother Richard III.

The Uncrowned King

Edward V (r.1483) was born in November 1470, during his father's brief exile to Holland. He was made prince of Wales on his father's return in 1471. His mother then accompanied him to Ludlow in 1473, where he became titular ruler of Wales and the Welsh Marches. He remained there for much of the rest of his father's reign.

When Edward became king in April 1483, his uncle Richard, duke of Gloucester, was appointed Protector. Conflict broke out between Gloucester and the Woodville nobles who had dominated the court of Edward IV. Richard arrested the Woodvilles and seized Edward and his younger brother, Richard, duke of York. The two princes were held in the Tower of London, which was then a royal residence as well as a prison.

THE PRINCES IN THE TOWER

The 'Princes in the Tower' were Edward V and Richard of Shrewsbury, duke of York, the two sons of Edward IV and Elizabeth Woodville. Edward V was a child when he became king in April 1483 so his uncle, Richard, duke of Gloucester, was appointed Protector. Shortly after Edward's coronation, Gloucester managed to hold the two boys captive in the Tower of London. An Act of Parliament of 1483, known as *Titulus Regius,* then declared the brothers illegitimate and awarded the crown to Gloucester. He ascended the throne as Richard III in July 1483.

There is no evidence of the princes having been seen after the summer of 1483. Their fate remains unknown – it is presumed that they either died in the Tower of London or they were killed there. During renovation work on the White Tower in 1674 the skeletons of two children were discovered under the staircase leading to the chapel. At that time, these remains were thought to have been those of the two princes. Charles II arranged their burial in Westminster Abbey. They were exhumed and examined in 1933, but by then it was too late to identify the corpses or establish the cause of death. But if the boys were indeed murdered, as was rumoured at the time, who was the culprit?

ABOVE *Missing, believed killed. The princes in the Tower disappeared while in the care of their uncle Richard III.*

Richard III is the most likely suspect. Although he had eliminated the princes from the succession, his hold on the monarchy was not secure. So the princes would have been a threat as long as they were alive. When the rumour that he had killed them circulated in late 1483, Richard never attempted to prove that they were alive by allowing them to be seen in public. Instead, he remained completely silent. He did not even order an investigation into their disappearance.

Then there is James Tyrrell, an English knight who was arrested by Henry VII's forces in 1501. He had offended the king by supporting another Yorkist claimant to the throne. Shortly before his execution, Tyrrell admitted that he had murdered the princes at the behest of Richard III. However, his confession was extracted under torture so it is therefore open to question.

Henry Stafford, duke of Buckingham, was Richard's right-hand man. But he was also a descendant of Edward III through John of Gaunt, duke of Lancaster, making him a claimant to the throne. That gave him several motives. He might have disposed of the princes on behalf of Richard or his fellow Lancastrian Henry Tudor. Or perhaps he murdered the princes to support his own claim.

When Henry VII came to the throne he found legal excuses to execute some of his rivals. His marriage to the princes' elder sister, Elizabeth of York, was a further way of reinforcing his claim. But Elizabeth's own claim depended on the death of both of her brothers. However, Henry's only opportunity to murder the princes would have been after his accession in 1485, when the two boys had already been missing for two years.

John Howard, claimant to the dukedom of Norfolk, is another suspect. He was given custody of the Tower of London on the night when the princes are thought to have disappeared. More than that, Richard, duke of York, was also the duke of Norfolk – he had inherited the title from his deceased child bride Anne. With Richard out of the way, the title went to John Howard.

The only suspect who actually went to trial was Richard III. He was found not guilty in a hearing presided over by three justices of the United States Supreme Court in 1997. Chief Justice William H. Rehnquist and Associate Justices Ruth Bader Ginsberg and Stephen G. Breyer came to the following unanimous decision: the prosecution had not proved that 'it was more likely than not' that the princes in the Tower had been murdered, nor had it shown that the bones found in 1674 were those of the princes. And it had not been established that Richard III had ordered, or was complicit in, their deaths.

Edward V's brief reign came to an end on 26 June when an assembly of the Lords and Commons ruled that the notoriously promiscuous Edward IV's marriage to Elizabeth Woodville was invalid. Consequently Edward V was illegitimate, leaving the way clear for Gloucester to be crowned Richard III.

The Last Yorkist King

Richard III (r.1483–5) was born on 2 October 1452 at Fotheringhay Castle in Northamptonshire. He had a claim to the English throne through both parents. His father was Richard Plantagenet, duke of York, and his mother was Cecily Neville. So it was inevitable that his family's conflict with Henry VI during the Wars of the Roses would dominate his early life. He was close to his brother, Edward IV. When Edward came to the throne in 1461 he created him duke of Gloucester. Richard shared his brother's exile in 1470 when Henry VI briefly returned to the throne, then he fought alongside Edward in his successful bid to regain his kingship.

When it was Richard's turn to be king, in June 1483, he was faced with a problem. His brother's two sons – the 12-year-old Edward V and his nine-year-old brother Richard, duke of York – were being held in the Tower. In August 1483, the two princes disappeared and the rumour spread that they had been murdered by Richard or his agents. A rebellion raised by the duke of Buckingham in October quickly collapsed and Buckingham was executed. However, the insurrection had eroded Richard's power base and people began to question his right to the crown.

In August 1485, Henry Tudor, earl of Richmond, a Lancastrian claimant to the throne, landed in South Wales. He marched eastwards and engaged Richard in battle on Bosworth Field on 22 August. Although Richard had the larger army, several of his key lieutenants defected. Refusing to flee, Richard was killed in battle and Henry Tudor took the throne as Henry VII (r.1485–1509).

Richard III is regularly depicted as England's most irredeemably evil king, who murdered his way to the throne. It was said that he was physically deformed, which was regarded as evidence of an evil character at the time. However, the physical features that have been attributed to him – the withered

BELOW *Richard III was not the club-footed hunchback that Shakespeare made out, though he almost certainly murdered his way to power.*

arm, the limp and the crooked back – are now thought to be literary fantasies. They perhaps originated in a questionable history written by Thomas More, a Tudor loyalist before he fell out with Henry VIII.

William Shakespeare also included Richard's so-called 'deformities' in his writings. But like Thomas More Shakespeare lived in the Tudor era – when it was politically correct to knock the Yorkists. In *Richard III,* Gloucester is portrayed as an ugly hunchback, who describes himself as 'rudely stamp'd' and 'deformed, unfinish'd'. In the same play, Richard orders the death of his brother George, duke of Clarence, and encourages Buckingham to murder the princes in the Tower. But there is no evidence to support the accusation that Richard was complicit in the death of Clarence. Indeed, once in power Richard is thought to have been a rather good king, who devoted his full attention to his duties, promoted trade and instituted financial reforms.

BELOW *Whatever his faults, Richard III faced death bravely on Bosworth Field, after key lieutenants had turned against him.*

CHAPTER FIVE

THE TUDORS

THE TUDORS

Henry VII (1485–1509)

Henry VIII (1509–47)

Edward VI (1547–53)

Lady Jane Grey (1553)

Mary I (1553–8)

Elizabeth I (1558–1603)

Dates show reign of monarch

LEFT *Martin Luther nails his '95 Theses' to the door of the Castle Church at Wittenberg, beginning the Protestant Reformation. At first, the Tudors had fought against Protestantism, but later embraced it.*

The Rise of the Tudors

Henry VII (r.1485–1509) was born on 28 January 1457 in Pembroke, Wales. His father, Edmund Tudor, who died nearly three months before he was born, was the son of a Welsh squire, Owen Tudor, and Catherine of Valois, widow of Henry V. An act of Parliament had been passed in 1428 which forbade Catherine to marry without the consent of the king and his council. Nevertheless Catherine bore Owen two daughters and three sons. This caused a scandal and in 1436 Owen Tudor was imprisoned. Catherine retired to Bermondsey Abbey in London, where she died shortly after giving birth in 1437. Owen was released, only to become a victim of the Wars of the Roses. He was captured after leading the Lancastrian force at the Battle of Mortimer's Cross in 1461, but he thought he would be spared because of his royal connections. Realizing that he was about to be beheaded, he murmured 'that hede shalle ly on the stocke that wass wonte to ly on Quene Katheryn's lappe'.

Fortunately for Henry VII his father, Edmund Tudor, was recognized and made earl of Richmond by Henry VI in 1452. Henry's mother Margaret of Beaufort, was the great-granddaughter of John of Gaunt, duke of Lancaster, whose children by Catherine Swynford were born before he married her. Richard II legitimated the union in 1397 and Henry IV repeated the process in 1407. However, the Beauforts were specifically excluded from the succession. This meant that Henry VII's claim to the throne was weak at best. That is, until the deaths of Henry VI and his son Prince Edward wiped out the direct line.

Because Margaret was only 14 years old when Henry VII was born she soon married again. So Henry was brought up by his uncle, Jasper Tudor, who fled with Henry to France after the Lancastrian defeat in 1471. By 1483, Henry had become the leading Lancastrian claimant to the English throne. His aid was sought by Buckingham when he rebelled against Richard III, but the rebellion was crushed before Henry could land in England. In December of the same year

BELOW *Henry Tudor was crowned Henry VII on the battlefield at Bosworth. He went on to unite the Yorkist and Lancastrian lines, ending the Wars of the Roses.*

he became betrothed to Elizabeth of York, the daughter of Edward IV. This united the opponents of Richard III.

In 1485, Henry landed at Milford Haven with 400 English exiles and a large contingent of French and Scottish troops. He marched on London, picking up support as he went. Richard had been waiting at Nottingham and the two armies met outside Market Bosworth. Although they were outnumbered, Henry's vanguard under the earl of Oxford fought well. Richard's fate was sealed when the earl of Northumberland and some of his other supporters failed to turn up. Then Lord Stanley, Margaret Beaufort's second husband and Henry's stepfather, switched sides at the last moment. Richard was slain and Henry was crowned on the battlefield with Richard's crown.

In January 1486, Henry married Elizabeth of York – after a dispensation from the pope because of their consanguinity. This act united the two sides in the Wars of the Roses. However, Henry's claim to the throne was all too shaky. The kingdom was full of dispossessed Yorkists and he was constantly plagued by conspiracies.

In 1486, Lord Lovell, Richard III's chamberlain, rose up against him, but he was easily crushed. In the following year, 12-year-old Lambert Simnel claimed to be Edward, earl of Warwick – the son of Richard III's elder brother, George, duke of Clarence. Simnel was crowned Edward VI in Dublin. Henry paraded the real earl of Warwick though the streets of London to no avail, because Simnel's support still grew.

In June 1487 Simnel landed in Lancashire with 2,000 German mercenaries provided by Edward IV's sister, Margaret of Burgundy. His army was swelled by around 4,000 Irish troops and 2,000 or so English followers.

Supported by John de la Pole, earl of Lincoln, Simnel marched towards London. Henry met the army at East Stoke near Newark in Nottinghamshire. Lincoln was killed and Simnel was captured. A priest named Richard Symonds, who had groomed Simnel for the role, was imprisoned but Henry recognized that Simnel was a harmless dupe. He was put to work in the royal kitchens, where he stayed until his death in around 1535.

In 1491, a second pretender, a Fleming named Perkin Warbeck, represented a somewhat greater threat to the throne. After arriving in Cork in 1491, elegant and handsome and dressed in fine

ABOVE *Edward, duke of Warwick, was rumoured to be dead. The pretender Lambert Simnel sought to steal his identity and ultimately the throne.*

ABOVE *The pretender Perkin Warbeck was put in the pillory on the orders of Henry VII and was later hanged.*

clothes, he was soon accepted as a person of royal descent. Margaret of York, duchess of Burgundy and sister of Edward IV, was deeply involved in the plot. She could well have trained him to impersonate Richard, her brother's younger son – one of the princes in the Tower.

Warbeck was also supported by Charles VIII (r.1483–98) of France, James IV (r.1488–1513) of Scotland and Maximilian I, king of Germany (r.1486–1513) and Holy Roman Emperor (r.1493–1519). Many powerful men in England also lent their support. After two abortive invasion attempts, in 1495 and 1496, the pretender landed in

Cornwall in 1497. Despite his army of 6,000 men, Warbeck fled at the sight of the king's forces. He found sanctuary in Beaulieu in Hampshire, where he was captured. Henry treated this second pretender as leniently as the first, but after he tried to escape from the Tower of London, he was hanged.

A further challenge to the throne came from Edmund de la Pole, earl of Suffolk, who was the eldest surviving son of Edward IV's sister Elizabeth and John de la Pole, duke of Suffolk. His elder brother, also named John, had been involved in the Simnel rebellion and the family lands had been confiscated after his death. Henry VII returned some of the lands to Edmund but he was made to forfeit the dukedom.

After being indicted for murder, Edmund fled to the Netherlands in 1499, where he sought the assistance of Margaret of Burgundy. He managed to gain the backing of Maximilian I, but Henry then made a treaty with Maximilian so Edmund was expelled. Having run out of support, Edmund was handed over to the English in Calais in 1506. He was finally executed in 1513. However, his brother Richard's claim to the throne of England was then recognized by Louis XII of France (r.1498–1515).

Henry consolidated his position with France through the Treaty of Étaples (1492). The treaty brought him a large indemnity, a handsome pension and the end of French support for Warbeck. He also concluded an alliance with Spain through the marriage of his eldest son, Arthur, to Catherine of Aragon, in 1501. Trade agreements with the Netherlands and the marriage of his daughter Margaret to James IV of Scotland in 1503 also cut off support for Perkin Warbeck.

By avoiding war, Henry rebuilt the royal finances and he reduced the power of the barons by taxing them heavily. He increased administrative efficiency, promoted trade and enforced royal fiscal rights to the point of ruthlessness. As a result, Henry was now wealthy in his own right, with a fortune of around £1.5 million pounds. The royal council was reinstituted as the Court of Star Chamber, which would deal with judicial matters. Henry sought to promote better order in Wales and the north by setting up special supervisory councils. Greater powers were entrusted to the justices of the peace and medieval rule, which was dominated by local law and custom, was gradually being eroded.

Under Henry VII, England was transformed into a single state that was subject to royal decree.

By the time he died on 21 April 1509, Henry had brought his country out of the Middle Ages and into the European Renaissance. He left a safe throne, a line that could not reasonably be challenged, a solvent government and a prosperous and united kingdom.

Supreme Head of the Church of England

Henry VII's eldest son Arthur died at an early age, so Henry was succeeded by his second son, Henry VIII (r.1509–47). Henry was born in Greenwich Palace on 28 June 1491. His brother had died in

BELOW *By avoiding war with his Continental neighbours, Henry VII ensured that England became a great power in Europe under his son, Henry VIII.*

IRELAND

Christopher Columbus crossed the Atlantic four times between 1492 and 1502, but it cannot be said that he discovered America. His intention was to discover a sea passage to the Orient. In 1492 he reached the Bahamas, which he thought was the Indies, so he called the people 'Indians'. The closest he got to America was during his third voyage in 1498, when he landed on the South American mainland. But he was still searching for the Orient.

However, his fellow Genoan Giovanni Caboto – known in England as John Cabot – had more success. Supported by Henry VII, he sailed from Bristol in May 1497 with the intention of finding a route to Asia. On 24 June he landed in what he thought was Asia – in fact it was Newfoundland. He then took possession of the land on behalf of England, by planting the Tudor flag. Cabot was lost on a second voyage in 1498.

The next century witnessed a surge in exploration. Sir Francis Drake plundered the Caribbean and explored the Pacific coast during his circumnavigation of the globe in 1577, while Sir Martin Frobisher went looking for a Northwest Passage in 1576, 1577 and 1578. In 1578 Sir Humphrey Gilbert received a six-year charter from Elizabeth I to settle 'heathen lands not actually possessed of any Christian prince or people', but his 1578 expedition was unsuccessful. On 3 August 1583, he claimed St John's, Newfoundland, for the Queen, but he was lost while returning to England.

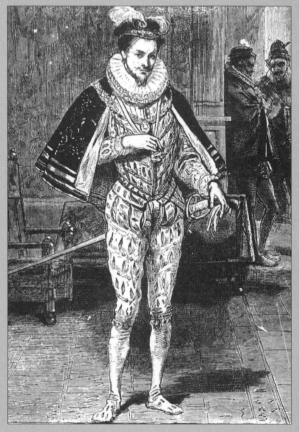

ABOVE *Sir Francis Drake plundered the Spanish treasure ships in the Caribbean. Then he rounded the Horn and attacked them in the Pacific.*

Then in 1585 and 1587 Sir Walter Raleigh tried to establish a colony near Roanoke Island, in present North Carolina. He named it Virginia, after Elizabeth I. The first group returned to England when their stores ran out but the 1587 colony disappeared without trace. In 1595, he led an expedition up the Orinoco, in the heart of the Spanish colonial empire, convinced that the fabulous golden city of Eldorado existed there. When he returned empty-handed some doubted him.

Elizabeth's successor James VI of Scotland disliked Raleigh. He was convicted of treason in 1603 and imprisoned in the Tower of London, where he wrote the first volume of his *History of the World* (1614). After 13 years, Raleigh was released to lead a second expedition to search for Eldorado. Not only was the expedition a failure, but Raleigh had defied the king's instructions by attacking the Spanish. On his return to England, Raleigh was sentenced to death and was executed on 29 October 1618.

In May 1607, the first permanent British settlement in North America was founded at Jamestown, in the mouth of the James River in Virginia. Named for James I of England, the colony cultivated tobacco and established the first representative government on the continent. The first Anglican church in America was built there and the first African slaves were brought ashore at Jamestown. In 1699, Virginia's seat of government was moved to Middle Plantation – later Williamsburg, which was named for William III. By then there were British colonies throughout New England and down the eastern seaboard.

ABOVE *Christopher Columbus landed on Cuba in 1492 and thought he had reached China. Five years later John Cabot claimed the 'new found land' of North America for England.*

RIGHT *Cardinal Wolsey, Henry VIII's lord chancellor, found it impossible to get the king a divorce from Catherine of Aragon. He was stripped of office.*

1502 so he had seven years in which to prepare himself for the role of king. An all-rounder, he excelled at book learning as well as jousting and the other physical pursuits of the aristocracy. Six feet (1.8 m) tall and powerfully built, great things were expected of him after his coronation in 1509. In the same year he married Catherine of Aragon, Arthur's widow, after obtaining a special dispensation from Pope Julius II.

Henry VII had left the royal coffers well filled, but his son's lavish entertaining soon depleted them. More interested in hunting, dancing and tennis than ruling, Henry increasingly relied on Thomas Wolsey, the priestly son of an Ipswich butcher. Wolsey had been chaplain to Henry VII and under Henry VIII he rose rapidly up the secular and clerical ladder. By 1515 he was both Lord Chancellor and a cardinal, his position superseding that of the archbishop of Canterbury. European power was then divided between France and the Holy Roman Empire, but Wolsey and Henry wanted to move its centre to England.

ABOVE *Catherine of Aragon was Henry VIII's first wife. When he was young, he loved her deeply. But she did not provide a son and heir.*

In 1512 Henry and his father-in-law Ferdinand II of Aragon (r.1479–1516) presented a united front against France. Wolsey organized the first French campaign and proved himself indispensable. He defeated the French at the Battle of the Spurs which took place at Guinegate in 1513. The victory was

known as the Battle of the Spurs because all that could be seen were the spurs of the French knights fleeing the field.

Later that year, Louis XII called on his ally, Henry's brother-in-law James IV of Scotland, to invade England, but the Scots were defeated at Flodden. However, Henry's war with France had proved expensive and ultimately unsuccessful, so in 1514 he made peace with Louis by marrying his sister Mary to him. Then in 1518 Wolsey drew up the Treaty of London. This was a non-aggression pact between all of the European powers – England, France, the Holy Roman Empire, the Papacy, Spain, Burgundy and the Netherlands. The success of the treaty brought glory on both Wolsey and his master Henry.

Although the peace did not last long it allowed Henry to build good relations with Louis VII's successor Francis I of France (r.1494–1547). They met outside Calais for two weeks of partying in June 1520. The most elaborate arrangements were made for the accommodation of the two monarchs and their large retinues. Henry's pavilion covered nearly two and a half acres (one hectare). Each king tried to outshine the other with huge feasts, music, jousting and games. Their dazzling tents and costumes displayed so much 'cloth of gold' – an expensive fabric woven with silk and gold thread – that the site of the meeting became known as the Field of the Cloth of Gold.

The event was seen as another of Wolsey's triumphs. However, such extravagance did not sit well with the English taxpayer and Henry became increasingly unpopular.

Wolsey's ascendancy was cut short by Henry's need for a male heir to secure the succession. The last thing England needed was a return to the Wars of the Roses, with rival factions fighting over the throne. Despite numerous pregnancies Queen Catherine had only managed to produce one child, Mary who had grown beyond infancy. It was feared that a female heir would bring uncertainty and possibly an end to the Tudor dynasty.

Henry became convinced that his marriage to Catherine – whom he had loved so dearly – was blighted because it was incestuous in the sight of God. She had previously been married to his brother. So he was determined to replace her with someone who could give him a son. But first his marriage had to be annulled. However, the pope refused to grant him a divorce. This was not surprising – Clement VII (in office 1523–34) was the prisoner of Catherine's nephew Charles V (r.1519–56), the Holy Roman Emperor, and Charles was not

BELOW *The middle-aged Henry VIII is entertained by Anne Boleyn, while Catherine of Aragon looks on. In fact, Anne held out while Henry pursued her.*

THE SPLIT WITH ROME

The English Church was established when Pope Gregory the Great (in office 590–604) sent Saint Augustine on a missionary expedition in 597. After Aethelberht, king of Kent, had been converted, many others followed. Saint Augustine then established his church in Canterbury, the former capital of Kent, and became the first archbishop of Canterbury.

Saint Columba established the Celtic Church in Iona in 563 and went on to evangelize Scotland and Ireland. The Celtic Church of North Britain submitted to the authority of Rome at the Synod of Whitby in 664 and the Greek Theodore of Tarsus, the seventh archbishop of Canterbury (in office 668–90), became the first archbishop to rule over the whole of the English Church. Over the next few centuries, the Roman system gradually absorbed the remaining Celtic Christian churches.

The English Church remained under papal authority for nearly a thousand years, before separating from Rome in 1534. A theological separation from Rome had been foreshadowed by various movements within the English Church, such as the Lollards, but the English Reformation gained political support when Henry VIII refused to submit to the authority of the pope. He had asked Pope Clement VII to sanction the annulment of his marriage to Catherine of Aragon, in order that he could marry Anne Boleyn. But under pressure from Catherine's nephew, the Emperor Charles V, Holy Roman Emperor, the pope refused Henry's request. Henry then took matters into his own hands. While remaining theologically a doctrinal Catholic, he became Supreme Head of the Church of England. He supported his action by issuing the 1534 Act of Supremacy. As a result, he was excommunicated by Pope Paul III (in office 1534–49) in 1538.

ABOVE *Pope Paul III refused to give Henry VIII a divorce from Catherine of Aragon. This forced Henry to break with Rome.*

Henry maintained a strong preference for the traditional Catholic ways during his reign, so few changes could be made to the practices of the Church of England. This indecisive phase led to Protestants being tried for heresy while Roman Catholics were penalized for not acknowledging Henry as Head of the Church of England.

Under Henry's son, Edward VI, Protestantism gained momentum with the issue of the new *Book of Common Prayer*. When Mary I came to the throne in 1553 the Church of England rejoined Rome, but her persecution of the Protestants aroused sympathy for their cause. Another dramatic change followed the coronation of Elizabeth I in 1558, because the Church of England split from Rome again. It then became mildly reformed, Catholic, apostolic and established — that is, it was both subject to the state and part of it. Its doctrines were spelt out in the '39 Articles' drawn up in 1571. However, religious disputes continued to cause great civil strife throughout the following century.

the sort of man you crossed. He had even famously sacked Rome in 1527.

All of the blame fell upon Wolsey's shoulders. In April 1530 he was stripped of office, after which he left for York. Then on 4 November, he was charged with treason. He died on his way to see the king and was replaced as chancellor by Sir Thomas More.

Henry divorced Catherine without the pope's permission and in 1533 he married Anne Boleyn. Her elder sister Mary had already given Henry a son. If the pope would not validate his actions

LEFT *Sir Thomas More refused to accept Henry VIII as head of the English Church and was executed in 1535. He became a saint 400 years later.*

Henry would take it upon himself. With the help of courtier Thomas Cromwell, and the 1534 Act of Supremacy, Henry established himself as Head of the Church of England. Henry's chancellor, Sir Thomas More, could not bring himself to go along with these arrangements. First of all he refused to attend the wedding of Henry and Anne and then he refused to take an oath recognizing Henry as Supreme Head of the Church of England. He was charged with treason, convicted on perjured evidence and sentenced to a traitor's death, that is, to be hanged, drawn and quartered. Henry mercifully commuted this to beheading. Thomas Cromwell then organized the dissolution of the monasteries in order to silence religious opposition and swell Henry's coffers. He also pushed through other major reforms of the 1530s – such as the uniting of England and Wales.

Like Catherine, Anne Boleyn also failed to give Henry a son. She produced only one daughter – the future Elizabeth I. In 1536 she was executed for treason on the grounds that she had been unfaithful to the king. Jane Seymour quickly took her

LEFT *Henry VIII married Anne of Cleves on the strength of Hans Holbein's portrait. In reality, the 'Flanders mare' was not to his taste.*

place as queen and in 1537 she successfully produced a male heir, who would become Edward VI. But Jane died only 20 days after giving birth.

Henry remained a staunch Catholic, despite his break with Rome – and despite the growing number of people at court, and in the nation, who now favoured Protestantism. In an attempt to establish a Protestant alliance with Germany, Cromwell arranged a marriage between the king and Anne of Cleves. Henry sent the court artist Hans Holbein the Younger to paint her picture. The artist returned with a flattering portrait. Swayed by the image, Henry married Anne by proxy in 1540. However, when she arrived in England

LEFT *Jane Seymour was the only one of Henry's six wives to give him a male heir. But he was a sickly boy and she died shortly after giving birth.*

PROTESTANTISM

Protestantism began as an attempt to reform the Western Christian Church in the 16th century. An initial feeling of discontent developed into the Protestant Reformation, which separated the reformed churches from the Roman Catholic Church. However, some authorities trace the beginnings of Protestantism back to the Waldensians in the 12th century. The Waldensians were the followers of the merchant Peter Waldo of Lyons, France, who practised what they believed to be the simple, uncorrupted Christianity of the primitive church. The movement, based in France and Italy, managed to survive violent official persecution. During the Reformation many Waldensians adopted Calvinism.

Then came Lollardy, a movement that began in the 1350s and was inspired by the teachings of the theologian John Wycliffe [see feature on page 81]. Wycliffe denied the authority of morally corrupted church prelates, rejected transubstantiation and other traditional teachings, and advocated biblical faith. The Lollards suffered persecution but survived to play a role in the English Reformation. The declared aim of the original reformers was to restore the Christian faith as it had been at its beginning, while retaining what they considered to be the better aspects of the Roman Catholic tradition.

A single event set in motion the tidal wave that was to become the Reformation. In 1517 Martin Luther nailed the '95 Theses' to the door of the Castle Church in Wittenberg. They attacked the indiscriminate sale of indulgences as a means of financing the construction of St Peter's Basilica in Rome. An indulgence was the remission of temporal punishment for sin. Luther, who was an Augustinian monk and a professor of theology at the University of Wittenberg, could see no justification for this in the Scriptures. The event might have gone unnoticed at an earlier date, but the invention of printing allowed the theses to be widely circulated. Luther was excommunicated, but he defended his views at the Diet of Worms in 1521. Although he was declared an outlaw, it was plain that he had powerful friends. Protected by Frederick III, elector of Saxony, he wrote a series of books and pamphlets. He began translating the Bible into the vernacular and his ideas spread rapidly throughout the states of Germany and elsewhere in Europe. In Scandinavia, Lutheran churches were quickly established.

Within a few years of Luther's rebellion an independent and more radical reform movement emerged in Zürich, Switzerland, under the leadership of the Swiss pastor Huldreich Zwingli. Zwingli's studies led him to the conclusion that nothing was binding or allowable unless it was commanded by the Bible and that the Gospels derived no authority from the Church. Zwingli's reforms were adopted peacefully by Zürich's town council and they soon spread to other Swiss cities.

At the second Diet of Speyer in 1529, the Roman Catholic majority attempted to withdraw the tolerance that had been granted to Lutherans at the Diet of 1526. A protest was signed by six Lutheran princes and the leaders of 14 free cities of Germany. After that Lutherans became known as Protestants.

The dominant reformer in the generation after Luther and Zwingli was John Calvin, a French theologian who settled in Geneva, Switzerland, in 1536. Calvin's ideas were not as radical as those of Zwingli, but life was austere for those within his sphere of influence. He used the Church and the State as the means of enforcing moral and doctrinal conformity. His follower John Knox introduced Calvinism into Scotland, where it became the established Presbyterian Church. Calvinism also spread to France, where its adherents were known as Huguenots, and to Holland, where it reinforced the Dutch determination to achieve independence from Catholic Spain.

Although England became Protestant at around the same time as the Continent, the move was not prompted by religious fervour. Henry VIII assumed ecclesiastical authority over the English Church merely because he wanted to annul his marriage to Catherine of Aragon and the pope would not give his permission. So in 1534 the Anglican Church became the established church. But Henry did not want to relinquish his old religion so he imposed severe laws that upheld the major tenets of medieval Catholicism. However, in 1563, during the reign of Elizabeth I, a distinctly English form of Protestantism was summarized by the '39 Articles'. Clergymen were ordered to subscribe to the Articles by Act of Parliament in 1571. Anglican ritual and church organization nevertheless retained many of the forms of Roman Catholicism, which drew it into conflict with the Calvinist-influenced dissenters known as Puritans.

Henry found that she was not at all to his taste. He called her his 'Flanders mare'. The divorce was amicable and was based on a plea of non-consummation. Henry gave evidence that Anne's ugliness had made him impotent. The fiasco was blamed on Cromwell, who was arrested and executed without trial.

The final years of Henry's reign witnessed his physical decline, coupled with his increasingly desperate attempts to recapture his earlier potency. In 1540, Henry married the youthful Catherine Howard, but it soon emerged that she had taken lovers before, and possibly during, their marriage. She was executed for treason within two years. A final marriage to Catherine Parr was more harmonious, although it was almost certainly platonic.

In his later years, Henry resumed his fruitless and expensive wars against Scotland and France. He also continued his father's work of creating a navy,

which he separated from the army for the first time. The first naval dockyard was established at Portsmouth where Henry built the 1,000-ton *Great Harry,* then the largest ship ever known. However, he had to endure the sight of his flagship, the *Mary Rose,* sinking before his eyes when she was manoeuvring in the Solent during a battle against the French in 1545. Henry died on 28 January 1547 and was succeeded by his only legitimate son, Edward.

ABOVE *Catherine Howard was a great beauty who took lovers before and possibly during her marriage. She paid with her life.*

LEFT *Catherine Parr was Henry's sixth and last wife. She had been widowed twice before he married her. After his death, she married her former suitor Thomas Seymour.*

PARVVLE PATRISSA, PATRIÆ VIRTVTIS ET HÆRES
ESTO, NIHIL MAIVS MAXIMVS ORBIS HABET.
GNATVM VIX POSSVNT COELVM ET NATVRA DEDISSE,
HVIVS QVEM PATRIS, VICTVS HONORET HONOS.
ÆQVATO TANTVM, TANTI TV FACTA PARENTIS,
VOTA HOMINVM, VIX QVO PROGREDIANTVR, HABENT
VINCITO, VICISTI. QVOT REGES PRISCVS ADORAT
ORBIS, NEC TE QVI VINCERE POSSIT, ERIT.

The Struggle for the Succession

Edward VI (r. 1547–53) was born on 12 October 1537 at Hampton Court Palace, which had been given to Henry VIII by Cardinal Wolsey. He was a frail, intellectual child, who excelled in Greek, Latin, French and theology. Edward was just nine years old when he came to the throne. His father had made arrangements for a regency council to rule on his behalf, but Edward's uncle, Edward Seymour, duke of Somerset, established himself as Protector. Somerset worked closely with Thomas Cranmer, the archbishop of Canterbury. The two men were intent upon hastening the English Reformation, with the help of the young king. The *Book of Common Prayer* was issued in 1549 – Latin had been used until then – and the Act of Uniformity of 1549 made it the sole legal form of worship in England.

Somerset was overthrown by the unscrupulous John Dudley, earl of Warwick and later duke of Northumberland. But the English Reformation was now in full swing. Cranmer issued a second *Book of Common Prayer* in 1552, altars were replaced with unadorned tables and religious imagery was destroyed. The new religious orthodoxy was enforced by a new and more stringent Act of Uniformity in 1552.

However, it soon became clear that Edward was suffering from tuberculosis and would not survive. Northumberland was determined that his religious reforms should not be undone, so he persuaded Edward to approve a new order of succession. This declared Catherine's daughter Mary and Anne Boleyn's daughter Elizabeth illegitimate. If nothing else, Mary was a devout Catholic. The throne was to pass to Northumberland's daughter-in-law, Lady Jane Grey, who was the great-granddaughter of Henry VII.

Edward died on 6 July 1553 and Jane was proclaimed queen four days later. However, Mary Tudor had generated widespread support by mid-July. So much so that Jane's father, the duke of Suffolk, abandoned his daughter and attempted to save himself by supporting Mary. Northumberland's supporters melted away and he was executed in that same year.

Jane, together with her father and her husband, Lord Guildford Dudley, were taken to the Tower of London. While Suffolk was pardoned, Jane and Dudley were tried for high treason in November 1553. Jane pleaded guilty and they were both sentenced to death. The sentence was suspended, but their fate was sealed by the actions of Jane's father. His support for a rebellion raised by Sir Thomas Wyatt in February 1554 brought about the execution of Jane and her husband. They were beheaded on 12 February and Suffolk was executed two days later.

OPPOSITE *A portrait of Edward VI, the boy-king who died from tuberculosis at the age of 15.*

BELOW *Lady Jane Grey was queen for just a few days in 1553 before being executed for high treason.*

A Brief Return to Catholicism

Mary I (r.1553–8) was born at Greenwich on 18 February 1516. She was the only surviving child of Henry VIII and Catherine of Aragon. After her half-sister Elizabeth was born, Mary was stripped of her title of princess and denied access to her parents. She never saw her mother again. With the death of Anne Boleyn there was a chance that she could be reconciled with the king, but Mary was a staunch Catholic and she refused to recognize her father as head of the Church. Eventually she agreed to submit to her father's will. She returned to the court where she was given her own household, as well as being named second in line to the throne after her younger brother Edward.

Mary made a triumphal entry into London within days of Edward's death in 1553. Once she was queen, she decided that marriage to Philip II of Spain would bring England back to the Catholic fold. But the English did not want a foreign king on the throne. The better-off also had a financial stake in a Protestant England. They had gained church lands and revenues after Henry had dissolved the monasteries and were loth to lose them.

In 1554 the peasants of Kent rose up against the foreign match. They were led by Sir Thomas Wyatt, who arrived at the outskirts of London with 3,000 men behind him. But they became disheartened when they entered the city and discovered that the populace did not want to join them. Confronted by the royal forces, Wyatt surrendered after a brief engagement. During his trial he dashed the hopes of the authorities by refusing to implicate Princess Elizabeth, a fellow Protestant. When Mary began persecuting Protestants at a later date, Wyatt and his followers were seen as martyred patriots.

Mary then married Philip, although he spent little time in the country. She pressed on with the restoration of Catholicism and revived the laws against heresy. It is thought that up to 300 Protestants were burned at the stake in Smithfield. Thomas Cranmer, the archbishop of Canterbury lost his life, along with other Protestant leaders. This purge earned Mary the nickname

'Bloody Mary'. Her marriage to Philip of Spain dragged England into an unsuccessful war against France which, in January 1558, led to the loss of Calais, England's last possession in France. Mary died on 17 November 1558, childless, sick and alone. Her hopes for a Catholic England died with her.

BELOW *Mary Queen of Scots lands in England to seek refuge. She was the Catholic cousin of the new queen, Elizabeth I, and the next in line to the throne.*

The Virgin Queen

Mary was succeeded as Queen of England and Ireland by her half-sister Elizabeth I (r.1558–1603). She was variously nicknamed 'Gloriana', 'the Virgin Queen' or 'Good Queen Bess'. Elizabeth was born in Greenwich on 7 September 1533, the only daughter of Henry VIII and his second wife, Anne Boleyn. When Anne was beheaded, Elizabeth was two years old. She was declared illegitimate and lost the title of princess. However, her governesses saw to it that she became highly educated.

It was a dangerous time for Elizabeth when her brother Edward died and her half-sister Mary became queen. Determined to re-establish Catholicism in England, Mary had viewed the Protestant Elizabeth as a direct threat. Elizabeth was briefly imprisoned in the Tower of London, although she was not excluded from the succession. When Elizabeth took the throne in 1558, her first priority was to return England to the Protestant faith. She also presided over a significant expansion in England's overseas trade and a flowering of the arts. Shakespeare, Spenser and Marlowe were staging a renaissance in poetry and drama at this time.

Catholic challenges and plots persisted through much of Elizabeth's reign. The focus of most of these intrigues was Elizabeth's Catholic cousin, Mary, Queen of Scots (r.1542–67). Mary's Tudor blood made her next in line to the English throne after Elizabeth but Roman Catholics believed that she was the lawful queen. They saw Henry VIII's divorce from Catherine of Aragon as invalid, making Elizabeth illegitimate. This position was supported by Mary's father-in-law, Henry II of France (r.1547–59). Henry's death in 1559 brought Mary's husband Francis II to the throne, but he died in the following year, leaving her a widow at the age of 18.

Mary returned to Scotland in 1561. However, while she had been away in France Scotland had reformed from Catholicism to Calvinism and she was seen as a foreign queen with an alien religion. In 1565, she married her cousin Henry Stewart, earl of Darnley. The marriage was not a happy one. A jealous man, Darnley murdered her secretary and confidant David Rizzio in front of her eyes and she feared for her own life. The birth of their son James did little to reconcile the couple.

After Darnley became ill he stayed at a house at Kirk o'Field on the outskirts of Edinburgh so that he could recover. On the night of 9 February 1567 there was an explosion and Darnley was strangled when he tried to escape the flames. Three months later Mary married James Bothwell, the chief suspect in Darnley's murder. The couple soon faced a rebellion. Mary's forces met the rebels at

OPPOSITE *Elizabeth I's 44-year reign brought much-needed stability to England and is now seen as a golden age of exploration and culture.*

BELOW *Henry Stuart, earl of Darnley, was Mary Queen of Scots' second husband and the father of her son, who went on to become James I of England.*

ABOVE *Lord Robert Dudley was a favourite of Elizabeth I. During Mary I's reign, they had been imprisoned together in the Tower of London. They were later rumoured to be lovers.*

OPPOSITE *This portrait of Elizabeth I was painted to celebrate the defeat of the Spanish Armada, which is shown in the background. Her hand rests on the globe, symbolizing England's global reach.*

Carberry Hill near Edinburgh on 15 June 1567, but she promised not to fight provided Bothwell was allowed to escape. Bothwell fled to the Shetland Isles and then to Denmark, where he died in prison in 1578. Mary was imprisoned on the tiny island of Loch Leven and was then deposed in favour of her one-year-old son James. She escaped in 1568 but her supporters were defeated at the Battle of Langside.

Mary then sought refuge in England, only to be imprisoned for the next 18 years by her cousin Elizabeth. She remained a focus for Catholic dissidents in England and was linked, rightly or wrongly, to a number of plots. In the end she was tried and convicted of being involved in the Babington Plot. Her execution took place in the great hall of Fotheringhay Castle in 1587.

Elizabeth's refusal to marry was the reason that Mary had remained a threat. Many royal suitors came forward. They included Philip of Spain, hoping to renew the Catholic hold on England; Archduke Charles of Austria; Erik XIV, king of Sweden; Henry, duke of Anjou, later king of France; and François, duke of Alençon. However, she rejected them all, unwilling to cede power to a husband, particularly a Catholic.

After being rejected as a suitor, Philip II of Spain launched the ill-fated Spanish Armada in an attempt to reimpose Catholicism on England by force. But Elizabeth was a popular monarch and a brilliant public speaker. She rallied the country and united it against the common enemy. The Armada was defeated.

Despite pressure from her advisers, particularly her chief secretary, William Cecil, Lord Burghley, Elizabeth preserved her independence by developing the cult of the Virgin Queen, although it is unlikely that she remained a virgin. Even before she came to the throne there was a rumour that she had been made pregnant by her guardian, the ambitious Thomas Seymour. He was the last husband of Henry VIII's widow Catherine Parr and many of his visits to Elizabeth had been made while his wife was alive. But Catherine died in 1548, which made Thomas' brother Edward, the Lord Protector, even more convinced that he intended to marry Elizabeth. Seymour was arrested and executed in 1549.

Elizabeth's name was also linked with that of Lord Robert Dudley, who had been imprisoned in the Tower with her, but his family had arranged his marriage to a wealthy heiress. His wife stayed in the country while Dudley spent his time in London with Elizabeth. But Dudley's wife was found dead in suspicious circumstances at the foot of the stairs in her Berkshire home. Elizabeth then had to keep her distance from Dudley, although he was later made earl of Leicester. Her next suitor was Sir William Pickering. He was followed by Sir Christopher Hatton, a handsome young lawyer from Northampton. Hatton was replaced by Thomas Heneage, a gentleman of the Queen's Privy Chamber, who was then followed by Edward de Vere, earl of Oxford, who showered her with gifts from his travels. Even Sir Walter Raleigh entered the

RIGHT *The story of Sir Walter Raleigh laying his cloak in the mud to prevent Elizabeth soiling her feet is thought to have been invented in the Victorian era to illustrate the chivalry of the age.*

BELOW *Robert Devereux, earl of Essex, was another of Elizabeth's favourites. She forgave his secret marriage and his subsequent adultery, but she would not forgive his rebellion.*

picture, until he seduced a lady of the bedchamber named Elizabeth Throckmorton. When Elizabeth discovered that they had married, she flew into a jealous rage and briefly imprisoned the couple in the Tower.

In later life Elizabeth fell for the young Robert Devereux, earl of Essex. However, he secretly married the widow of Sir Philip Sidney. Even though Elizabeth allowed him to return to court, he began pursuing other ladies-in-waiting. The queen eventually forgave Essex his adulterous escapades, but she could not afford to be so generous when, in 1599, he was accused of spreading sedition in Ireland. However, she stopped short of sending him to trial for treason and instead had him severely censured in a private court of justice.

Unrepentant, Essex and a small band of followers rode into London with a plan to capture the Tower, raise support in the City and then seize the queen. But she was safely barricaded in the Palace of Westminster and support for the rebellion quickly dwindled. Essex made a last stand at his London mansion but he was forced to surrender. He was finally convicted of high treason and sentenced to death.

Even then the queen might have saved him. She had once given him a ring which, she had promised, would absolve him of any crime. He sent it to her but on its way it fell into the hands of one of his enemies, Lady Nottingham. She held on to it until it was too late, only passing it to the queen after Essex had been beheaded.

Despite all this Elizabeth had asked Parliament to erect 'a marble stone [that] shall declare that a Queen, having reigned such a time, lived and died a virgin'. No such monument was ever built. On her deathbed, on 23 March 1603, Elizabeth named her cousin the Protestant James VI of Scotland (r.1567–1625) – the son of Mary, Queen of Scots – as her heir. Beside Elizabeth as she died was a small casket containing the last letter she had received from Robert Dudley.

THE SPANISH ARMADA

The defeat of the Spanish Armada is one of the most famous events in English history. It was arguably Queen Elizabeth's finest hour. Even beforehand, she had been hailed as the saviour of the English people. She now lived up to her image by defeating Spain, the greatest power of the 16th century. Philip II of Spain ruled vast territories and derived unparalleled wealth from the New World, while England was a small country, with little wealth, few friends and many enemies.

The hostility between England and Spain was no secret. England was a Protestant country while the Spaniards were fervent Catholics. The Spanish believed that Elizabeth was illegitimate and had no right to the English throne. There had even been Spanish plots to oust her. Elizabeth had encouraged the activities of the English pirates who plundered Philip's ships as they made their way home from the New World. This had angered Philip immensely. Even worse, the stolen treasure funded the Protestants who rebelled against his rule in the Spanish-held Netherlands.

Philip believed that he had a genuine claim to the English throne. He could claim descent from John of Gaunt and he had been the husband of Mary I. When Mary died in 1558, Philip was unwilling to let his precarious hold on England slip away, so he proposed marriage to Elizabeth. The queen was a master of procrastination. She protested her friendship to Philip's face but encouraged pirates such as Sir John Hawkins and Sir Francis Drake behind his back. They were out seizing Spanish ships and goods in the West Indies with her full knowledge.

ABOVE *Sir Francis Drake had a formidable career as a privateer – a state-sponsored pirate – before provoking the Spanish further by an attack on the port of Cádiz.*

As early as 1585, Philip had begun to prepare a great fleet for the invasion of England. It was to be commanded by the Marquis of Santa Cruz, but after his death in 1586 the Duke of Medina Sidonia was put in charge. At first the Armada was going to be used to liberate Mary, Queen of Scots and put her on the throne. But when Mary was executed in 1587 for conspiring against Elizabeth, Philip planned to invade England in the name of his daughter, the Infanta Isabella. The purpose of the new mission was to depose Elizabeth and make England Roman Catholic once again.

But Medina Sidonia did not have a naval background. In fact, he had no interest in leading the Armada, as the invasion fleet came to be called. Once on board he became seasick and begged to be relieved from duty, but Philip ignored the request.

The Armada took some time to assemble because ships from the Mediterranean had to be re-rigged if they were to sail across the Bay of Biscay and up the English Channel. Despite the Spaniards' precautions, the English were well aware of their preparations. In a bold move, Sir Francis Drake sailed a small English fleet to Cádiz, where he burned and sunk a number of warships, slipping away before the Spanish could retaliate. Although this was more of an annoyance than a setback to the Spanish, the English took heart from this 'singeing of the King of Spain's beard'.

THE SPANISH ARMADA continued

By May 1588, the Armada was finally ready to sail. It numbered over 130 ships, making it by far the greatest naval fleet of its age. According to Spanish records, 30,493 men sailed with the Armada, the vast majority of them soldiers. However, many of the Spanish vessels were converted merchant ships, better suited to carrying cargo than fighting at sea. They were broad and heavy, and could not manoeuvre quickly under sail.

The Spanish did not see this as a problem because they did not intend to engage the English in a sea battle. They regarded their ships as troop transports, whose job it was to land men and armaments at designated points around the coast. The Spanish were regarded as the best soldiers in Europe at the time, so they thought they would have the advantage, both on land and at sea. It was common for ships to draw alongside each other so that fighting men could engage in hand to hand combat. However, Hawkins, Drake and the other privateers that plundered the Caribbean had developed new tactics. In particular, they had become skilled in the use of naval artillery.

The Spanish plans called for the Armada to sail up the English Channel and then meet up with the Duke of Parma near Dover. He headed the Spanish forces in the Netherlands and his men were to join the invasion force. But communications were slow and the logistical problems of a rendezvous at sea were immense. The Duke of Parma had little faith in Medina Sidonia or the invasion plan and so he kept his co-operation to a minimum. Philip himself was also of little help. He issued a steady stream of commands, but he seldom met his commanders. And he never let his experienced military leaders develop their own tactics. Although he had little military experience, Philip believed that he was guided by God so his mission was bound to succeed.

Things were far better organized in England. A series of signal beacons had been set up on the hills that fringed the English and the Welsh coasts. When the Spanish ships appeared off the Lizard on 19 July 1588 all the beacons were lit, so that news of the Armada raced through the realm. The English ships then slipped out of their harbour at Plymouth under cover of darkness and managed to get behind the Spanish fleet.

While the English sailors engaged the Armada, Elizabeth I rode to Tilbury. Sitting on her white horse she addressed her troops with the following words:

'My loving people, we have been persuaded by some that we are careful of our safety, to take heed how we commit ourselves to armed multitudes for fear of treachery; but, I do assure you, I do not desire to live to distrust my faithful and loving people. Let tyrants fear, I have always so behaved myself, that under God I have placed my chiefs' strength and safeguard in the loyal hearts and goodwill of my subjects; and, therefore, I am come amongst you as you see at this time, not for my recreation and disport, but being resolved, in the midst and heat of battle, to live or die amongst you all – to lay down for my God, and for my kingdoms, and for my people, my honour and my blood even in the dust. I know I have the body of a weak and feeble woman; but I have the heart and stomach of a king – and of a king of

ABOVE *While the English fleet attacked the Armada, Elizabeth I rode to Tilbury to address her troops.*

England too, and think foul scorn that Parma or Spain, or any prince of Europe, should dare to invade the borders of my realm; to which, rather than any dishonour should grow by me, I myself will take up arms – I myself will be your general, judge, and reward of every one of your virtues in the field. I know already, for your forwardness, you have deserved rewards and crowns, and, we do assure you, on the word of a prince, they shall be duly paid you. For the meantime, my Lieutenant-General Leicester shall be in my stead, than whom never prince commanded a more noble or worthy subject; not doubting but by your obedience to my General, by your concord in the camp, and your valour in the field, we shall shortly have a famous victory over these enemies of my God, of my kingdom and of my people.'

The Spanish fleet sailed up the Channel in a crescent formation, with the troop transports in the centre. They reached Plymouth on 19 July 1588 and were surprised to find a large contingent of English ships waiting for them. Lord Howard of Effingham, who commanded the English fleet, had fortunately taken the decision to protect the southwest coast from a Spanish landing force. At that point all the beacons were lit, carrying the news of the invasion as far as London.

But Medina Sidonia had now been instructed to meet the Duke of Parma at Calais before making a final assault on England, so the Armada sailed to its rendezvous point and dropped anchor.

ABOVE *The Spanish fleet swept up the English Channel in a crescent formation to protect the troop ships in the centre. But the army they carried would never land.*

The English fleet was right behind. On 28 July Effingham ordered a number of fire ships to be set adrift as night fell, so that the tide would carry the blazing vessels into the massed Spanish fleet. Many Spanish vessels scattered in the ensuing confusion.

On Monday, 29 July, the two fleets met in battle off Gravelines. The English emerged victorious, although the Spanish losses were not great – only three ships were reported sunk, one was captured and four more ran aground. Nevertheless, the Duke of Medina Sidonia decided that the Armada should return to Spain. The English blocked the Channel, so that the only route open was around the north of Scotland.

It was then that the unpredictable English weather took a hand in the proceedings. A succession of storms scattered the Spanish ships, resulting in heavy losses. By the time the remains of the Armada reached Spain, it had lost half of its ships and three-quarters of its men. The storms that scattered the Armada were seen as an intervention by God, a sign of divine approval for the Protestant cause. Services of thanks were held throughout the country, and a commemorative medal was struck, which bore the words, 'God blew and they were scattered'.

The queen's joy was marred by sorrow. Robert Dudley, who had been her companion since her accession, had died unexpectedly shortly after sharing the victory. Elizabeth went into seclusion. Dudley had left her some pearls in his will and it is said that she wore them in the official portrait that was painted to commemorate England's victory over the Armada.

Despite her grief, Elizabeth attended the victory celebrations at St Paul's. Although King Philip sent other fleets against England in the 1590s, none was as threatening as the great Armada of 1588.

CHAPTER SIX VI

THE STUARTS

THE STUARTS

James I (1603–25)

Charles I (1625–49)

The English Civil Wars (1642–51)

Republic – Commonwealth of England (1649–60)

Oliver Cromwell – Lord Protector (1653–8)

Richard Cromwell – Lord Protector (1658–9)

Charles II (1660–85)

James II (1685–8)

William III (1689–1702) with **Queen Mary II** (1689–94)

Queen Anne (1702–14)

Dates show reign of monarch

LEFT *Sir Walter Raleigh was beheaded in 1618 at the request of the Spanish ambassador, for engaging in hostilities with the Spanish against the instructions of James I to keep the peace.*

A Scottish King

When Elizabeth I died childless she handed the crown to James VI of Scotland (r.1567–1625), who became James I of England

RIGHT *James I of England, VI of Scotland, was known for his flamboyant dress and his numerous male favourites.*

(r.1603–25). After Elizabeth, all the kings and queens of England could call themselves monarchs of Great Britain.

James was the child of the doomed match between Mary, Queen of Scots and Lord Darnley, who was murdered early in 1567 when James was just eight months old. He was born on 19 June 1566 at Edinburgh Castle. Mary was forced to abdicate in favour of her son when he was only 13 months old and the infant king was placed on the Scottish throne on 24 July 1567. His mother left Scotland in May 1568 and never saw her son again.

John Knox, the Reformation leader, preached the sermon at James' coronation, thereby establishing his credentials as a Protestant monarch. James' childhood was turbulent – his minority was marred by a succession of regents as well as civil war. A more positive influence came in the form of his tutor, the Scottish humanist George Buchanan, who arranged his education in Greek, Latin, French, the classics and religious writings.

Before James was 12 years old, nominal power came into his hands when the earl of Morton was driven from the regency in 1578. But he then became the puppet of other factional leaders. After falling into the hands of the Catholic duke of Lennox, who hoped to win Scotland back for Mary, James was kidnapped in 1582 by William Ruthven, first earl of Gowrie. Ruthven forced James to denounce Lennox but the young king escaped his Protestant captors in 1583. James then established himself as a political figure in his own right when he signed the Treaty of

Berwick with Elizabeth I in 1586. The treaty created a bond between England and Scotland and pledged mutual help against invasion. In particular, it protected England from a back door onslaught by France. Consequently James could only make a formal protest over his mother's execution and he remained neutral when the Spanish Armada threatened English shores.

As the king of Scotland he signed an act of parliament that made him the head of the Presbyterian Church in Scotland. He then subdued the Roman Catholic earls. In 1589, he married Anne of Denmark. They had nine children, although it was noted that James generally preferred male company.

When Elizabeth I died in 1603, James immediately headed south to London. At the age of only 37 he was able to tell the English Parliament that he was 'an old and experienced king'. However, the English were outraged by his flamboyant attire and his open affection for good-looking young male favourites, who were often rewarded with titles, estates and advantageous marriages. James had overseen the persecution of witches in Scotland, where many were burnt. In England, he passed the draconian Witchcraft Act of 1604, which remained on the statute book until 1736. However, witchcraft was not taken seriously in England and juries would rarely convict. Some individuals faced the death penalty for witchcraft during the breakdown of law and order that accompanied the Civil War, but in England they were hanged, rather than burned.

James was generally regarded as an alien in England and his strong opinions earned him a reputation for narrow-mindedness and intellectual bullying. A stream of instructive texts flowed from his pen. He wrote two works between 1597 and 1598, in which he established

an ideological base for monarchy – *The Trew Law of Free Monarchies* and *Basilikon Doron* (the Royal Gift). In the *Trew Law,* he sets out the divine right of kings and explains that for biblical reasons kings are higher beings than other men. The document proposes an absolutist theory of monarchy which states that a king may impose new laws by royal prerogative but must also pay heed to tradition and to God. *Basilikon Doron* was written as a book of instruction for his eldest son, the four-year-old Prince Henry. Accordingly, it provides a more practical guide to kingship, in which James foreshadows his difficulties with

ABOVE *Scottish Protestant reformer John Knox brought Calvinism to Scotland and James became head of the Presbyterian Church. As a Protestant, he could take the English throne.*

IRELAND

With the accession of James VI of Scotland to the English throne in 1603, the two crowns were united and the king or queen of Scotland also became the monarch of England. Early on in its history, Scotland was occupied by five different peoples. They were the Picts, the Scots, the Angles, the ancient Britons and the Vikings. The Picts lived in the area north of the rivers Forth and Clyde, while the Scots, who were from Ireland, settled in Argyll in the 5th and 6th centuries. Lothian was held by the Angles and the ancient Britons had retreated to Strathclyde. Finally, in the 9th century, the Vikings settled in Orkney, Shetland, Caithness, Sutherland and the Western Isles.

The unification of these different peoples began in the mid-9th century, when Kenneth MacAlpin became king of both the Picts and Scots, reigning as Kenneth I (r.*c.*843–58). After that the Scots gradually took over, although the Vikings remained powerful in the Northern Isles of Orkney and

ABOVE *Kenneth I (top left) united the Picts and Scots in the 9th century. Duncan I (top right) had been ruler of Strathclyde before he became king of Scotland. Malcolm III Canmore (bottom left), Duncan's son, returned from exile in England to kill Macbeth (bottom right), his father's murderer.*

Shetland until the end of the Middle Ages. Little is known about the early kings up to the end of the 11th century, except that they usually took the crown by force. The three best-known kings of the century – Duncan I (r.*c.*1034–40), Macbeth (r.1040–57) and Malcolm III Canmore (r.1058–93) – were immortalized in Shakespeare's play *Macbeth,* but his depiction of them bears little resemblance to historical events.

At the start of the 12th century, Scotland saw a religious revival under David I (r.1124–53), the youngest of Malcolm Canmore's six sons to become king. More English than his predecessors, he had spent much of his early life at the court of Henry I. After taking over from his brother Alexander I (r.1107–24), he organized the building of 20 monasteries and improved the administration by granting town charters and introducing the first Scottish royal coinage. David also brought about the close relationship of the Scottish kings with the English court, which was reinforced by marriage. This led to the expansion of English as the language of government and the rise of the Anglo-Norman aristocracy in Scotland.

By the end of the 13th century there was no clear successor to Alexander III (r.1249–86). The resulting quarrels among Scottish nobles led to the intervention of Edward I of England. Sir William Wallace rebelled against the English, winning an important battle at Stirling Bridge in 1297. Wallace was eventually captured and executed in London in 1305, but he had started a conflict that dragged on for the next 300 years.

After the death of William Wallace, Robert the Bruce (r.1306–29), descendant of one of the original contestants for the Scottish throne, took up the struggle for Scotland's independence. He claimed the throne of Scotland in 1306 and his position was secured by his resounding victory at Bannockburn in 1314 and the Declaration of Arbroath in 1320.

The Stuart dynasty descended from Robert the Bruce's grandson Robert II (r.1371–90). He was the son of Robert I's daughter Marjory and her husband, Walter Stewart. The name Stewart became Stuart in the 16th century, when Scotland was influenced by France. The Stewart family was dogged by early death and seven Stewart kings succeeded as minors. Nevertheless, the dynasty flourished for over three centuries. Under their rule, Scotland moved forward to become a modern and prosperous nation.

The crowns of Scotland and England were united when James IV of Scotland (r.1488–1513) married Princess Margaret Tudor, daughter of King Henry VII of England. Their union, which took place at Stirling Castle in 1503, was known as the 'Marriage of the Thistle and the Rose'. However, the direct male line came to an end with the death of James V (r.1513–42). He was survived by only one legitimate child – Mary, Queen of Scots (r.1542–67). She, in turn, was succeeded by her only son James VI of Scotland (r.1567–1625), who went on to become James I of England in 1603.

the English House of Commons. 'Hold no Parliaments,' he tells Henry, 'but for the necesitie of new Lawes, which would be but seldome.' In 1604 he also published *A Counterblaste to Tobacco*, condemning the new habit of smoking. On top of all that he wrote poetry.

James' radical Presbyterianism was particularly opposed by English Catholics, who made an attempt on his life in 1605, during the episode known as the Gunpowder Plot. He oversaw a new English translation of the Bible in 1611. It would be the standard text for more than 250 years. In 1612, James had his mother's body taken from its original place of burial at Peterborough Cathedral and placed in a vault in King Henry VIII's Chapel, Westminster Abbey.

James had been forced to conclude a peace with Spain in 1604 after Parliament had withdrawn its funding for the Anglo-Spanish War. His often extravagant expenditure was opposed at every turn. Unable to reach a settlement, James dissolved Parliament in 1611. In 1614, he recalled Parliament – it was called the 'Addled Parliament' because it was so ineffective – but dissolved it again after eight weeks when it refused to grant him the money he required. He then sought money by attempting to marry his son Charles, who was prince of Wales following the death of Prince Henry in 1612, to the Spanish Infanta. Sir Walter Raleigh was a casualty of James' Spanish hopes – he was executed in 1618 at the request of the Spanish ambassador. However, James' policy of détente with the Spanish foundered when his Protestant son-in-law Frederick V, Elector Palatine, accepted the formerly Catholic crown of Bohemia in 1619. Frederick only lasted for a year, but his action provoked a Spanish invasion and marked the beginning of the Thirty Years' War.

ABOVE *James had been the scourge of witches in Scotland. But in England people did not take witchcraft seriously and juries would rarely convict.*

James called another parliament in 1621, but it refused to grant him funds to mount an expedition in support of Frederick. Recalling how much Elizabeth had gained from looting the Spanish, Parliament now urged James to declare war on Spain. They also sought to ban Charles from marrying a Catholic, further cooling relations between Parliament and the Crown.

However, James did have some successes. Under his reign England established its first successful colonies on the American mainland – Virginia,

Massachusetts and Nova Scotia. There had been Jamestown in 1607 and the Pilgrim Fathers sailed from Plymouth in 1620. In 1624, King James wrote his *Evangelistic Grant Charter* to settle the Colony of Virginia:

'To make habitation... and to deduce a colony of sundry of our people into that part of America, commonly called Virginia... in propagating of Christian religion to such people as yet live in darkness... to bring a settled and quiet government.'

THE GUNPOWDER PLOT

ABOVE *With the Parliament building on the riverside, it was easy for the conspirators to bring in the gunpowder to conceal in the cellar.*

In 1605 a group of English Catholics conspired to blow up the Houses of Parliament during the state opening on 5 November, at which the new king James I, his queen and his heir would be present. The five original conspirators – Guy Fawkes, Robert Catesby, Thomas Winter, John Wright and Thomas Percy – were angry that James had refused to grant religious toleration to Catholics. Their plan was to take over the country in the inevitable confusion that would follow the assassination of the king and his ministers.

As part of their plan, they rented a cellar that extended under the old Parliament building. After Fawkes had concealed over twenty barrels of gunpowder the conspirators separated until the fateful day. Feeling the need to broaden the conspiracy, Catesby told his cousin Francis Tresham about their plans. He in turn warned his Catholic brother-in-law Lord Monteagle not to attend Parliament on 5 November. Monteagle alerted the Government and Fawkes was apprehended in the cellar on the night of 4 November. He was tortured until he revealed the names of the other conspirators. Their number had now reached ten.

Catesby, Percy and Wright were killed while resisting arrest. Others, perhaps less fortunate, were tried and sentenced to be hanged, drawn and quartered. Robert Winter, Thomas Bates, John Grant and Sir Everard Digby were put to death near St Paul's Churchyard on 30 January 1606. On the following day Thomas Winter, Ambrose Rookwood, Robert Keyes and Guy Fawkes were executed in Old Palace Yard, in front of the Houses of Parliament.

As a result of the plot, the recusancy law that fined those who refused to attend Anglican services was strictly enforced and the Observance of 5th November Act was passed. This made it compulsory to celebrate the arrest and execution of Guy Fawkes every 5 November. It stayed in force in England and its dominions until 1859.

James suffered from ill-health and depression after the early death of Prince Henry in 1612 and the loss of his wife Anne in 1619. He survived numerous attempts on his life but when he died on 27 March 1625 it was rumoured that he had been poisoned by George Villiers, the first duke of Buckingham. Villiers had practically run the country in James' final years. A post-mortem merely confirmed that James' physical state had been poor.

He was suffering from a host of diseases. His enlarged heart was soft. He had kidney stones, blackened lungs and a brain so swollen that it oozed out of his skull when the embalmer began his grisly work.

ABOVE *George Villiers, duke of Buckingham, was a favourite of James I and his son Charles I, and practically ran England for a time.*

The English Civil War

James I was succeeded by his second son Charles I (r.1625–49), who was born in Fife on 19 November 1600. Three months after his accession Charles married Henrietta Maria, daughter of Henry IV of France (r.1589–1610). They had a happy marriage which resulted in five surviving children. However, because Henrietta Maria was a Catholic she was disliked by Parliament.

Charles was unpopular from the start because of his friendship with George Villiers, duke of Buckingham, who had become even more powerful with the accession of the young king. It was Buckingham who had attempted to organize the marriage of Charles to the Spanish Infanta in 1623. When that ploy foundered he arranged Charles' marriage to Henrietta Maria, but he failed to use it to secure an Anglo-French alliance. At the same time, Parliament was alarmed by the threat of a Catholic succession. Buckingham then organized an expensive and failed campaign against Cádiz in October 1625. When Parliament sought to impeach him, Charles had the House dissolved. Buckingham was tried before the Royal Court of the Star Chamber instead but to no one's surprise he was found not guilty.

Britain was drifting into war with France at that point. In June 1627 Buckingham took command of 8,000 men and went off to relieve the Huguenots who were under siege by French government troops at the port of La Rochelle. The campaign was a disaster and Buckingham returned to Portsmouth that November with just 3,000 men. The parliament of 1628 tried to pressure Charles into dismissing his favourite. However, the king encouraged Buckingham to launch another expedition in August. But while he was assembling a fresh fleet at Portsmouth, Buckingham was stabbed to death by John Felton, a naval lieutenant, who claimed he was doing the will of Parliament. The people of London rejoiced when they heard the news of Buckingham's death.

Charles' habit of regularly dissolving Parliament had increased his money troubles. Buckingham's foreign adventures had also depleted his coffers. On top of that, his preference for the High Anglican form of worship, and his Catholic wife, alienated many of his subjects – not least the growing number of Puritans. In 1629, Charles dismissed Parliament once again and resolved to rule alone for the next 11 years. This forced him to raise revenue by non-parliamentary means. He imposed customs duties at a time of expanding trade and increased traditional crown dues. At the same time, he initiated a crackdown on Puritans and Catholics, many of whom emigrated to America.

Charles also alienated the Scottish Calvinists by attempting to force a new prayer book on the country, based on the *Book of Common Prayer*. In 1638 many Scots signed the National Covenant to defend the Presbyterian religion. Charles, himself a Scot, declared war on Scotland but by March 1639 he found himself beaten in the First Bishops' War. He needed to raise funds to continue the fight so he was forced to summon Parliament again on 13 April 1640. But he refused to listen when the House insisted on discussing grievances. He dismissed the so-called Short Parliament on 5 May and the Scottish Covenanter army crossed the border in August. The king's troops fled before a cannonade at Newburn, which allowed the Scots to march into Newcastle. Charles was forced to convene the Long Parliament at Westminster in November 1640. It sat until at least April 1653, although it might not have been legally dissolved until March 1660.

The assembly passed the Triennial Act in 1641, which ensured that Parliament met at least once every three years. It

also impeached Charles' unpopular adviser and lord deputy in Ireland, the earl of Strafford. Despite Charles' intervention, Strafford was beheaded in May 1641. Charles was then forced to concede that Parliament could not be dismissed against its will. Parliament also condemned his tax-raising methods. In August the king headed for Scotland, hoping to raise support.

When Parliament reconvened in November 1641 the House of Commons passed the Grand Remonstrance, which condemned almost everything that Charles had done since he had come to

ABOVE *Charles I married Henrietta Maria, daughter of Henry IV of France and a Catholic. They had four sons and five daughters.*

BELOW *The fort at La Rochelle where Huguenots, French Protestants, were besieged. Buckingham went to their aid but, after four months, was forced to withdraw.*

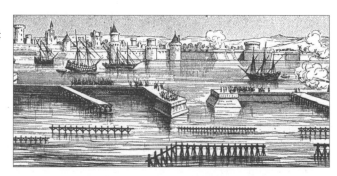

ABOVE *Oliver Cromwell at the Battle of Marston Moor on 2 July 1644.*

could well be used against them. So the Commons asked Charles to sign a militia bill that would give them command of the army. He replied, 'By God, not for an hour.' Charles also began to fear that the strongly Puritan Parliament might impeach his Catholic queen. In an effort to intimidate them he ordered the arrest of one member of the House of Lords and five members of the Commons on a charge of treason. Charles led a force of some 400 men into Westminster but all of the MPs had escaped.

In January 1642, Charles left for the north of England while Henrietta Maria sailed for Holland, where she pawned the crown jewels to raise money for her husband. The king then settled in York, where a group of royalist MPs joined him. Those who had remained at Westminster sent him a list of demands – the '19 Propositions'. Among other things, the army was to be placed under parliamentary control, ministers could only be appointed with Parliament's approval and Parliament should decide the future of the Church. While Charles was careful not to dismiss this ultimatum out of hand, both sides prepared for war. The royal standard was raised in Nottingham on 22 August 1642 and the Civil War began.

In September 1642 the earl of Essex, leading the parliamentary forces, left London for the Midlands, while Charles moved his headquarters to Shrewsbury. On 23 October, the two sides met at Edgehill near Warwick. The battle was inconclusive. Charles gained the advantage on the field, which enabled him to advance on Oxford, Aylesbury and Reading. Essex managed to rally the parliamentary forces at Turnham Green, which prevented the king from taking London. Charles then withdrew to Oxford, which remained his capital for the rest of the war.

the throne. News then came of a rebellion in Ireland. Parliament was wary of letting Charles raise an army to suppress the uprising, fearing that it

In the following year, the royalists won control of Yorkshire and the southwest after Charles' nephew, Prince Rupert, captured Bristol. The queen arrived with shiploads of arms from Holland and plans were laid to make a three-pronged attack on London from Oxford, Yorkshire and the west. However, the men from Yorkshire and the West Country were unwilling to fight outside their areas. After Charles had turned down its tentative peace offer, Parliament struck an alliance with the Scottish Covenanter army. For his own part Charles concluded a peace in Ireland, which freed up a number of his troops. The Scottish army crossed the border in January 1644, throwing Charles on the defensive. This time it was his turn to have an offer of peace rejected.

In December 1644, Oliver Cromwell, general of the parliamentary forces, made a speech arguing that Parliament could not win the Civil War unless the army was improved. As a result the New Model Army was organized under Sir Thomas Fairfax in February 1645. On 14 June, this highly disciplined force proved its worth when it overcame Charles and Prince Rupert at the battle of Naseby near Leicester. Further royalist defeats followed. Charles withdrew to Oxford in November and by the spring of 1646 he was surrounded there.

In April Charles left the city in disguise and made his way to the camp of the Scottish Covenanter army in Newark. But the covenanters had made peace with the English Parliament and they handed Charles over to the parliamentary commissioners when they left England in January 1647. Charles was initially held in Northamptonshire but he was eventually moved to the headquarters of the New Model Army at Newmarket. From there he was taken to Hampton Court. He escaped, planning to make his way to Jersey and then France, but he was recaptured by the parliamentarians and taken to Carisbrooke Castle on the Isle of Wight. Charles then began a series of negotiations with Parliament, the leaders of the New Model Army and the Scots.

In December 1647, Charles came to a secret agreement with the Scots in which he promised to establish Presbyterianism in England if they returned him to power. The Scots invaded England in July 1648 and royalist rebellions broke out, starting the Second Civil War. The last of Charles' Scottish supporters were defeated at the Battle of Preston in August 1648 and the remaining English rebellions were suppressed. Convinced that there would never be peace while the king lived, a rump of radical MPs, including Cromwell, put Charles on trial for treason and other high crimes against the realm of England. His chief offence was prosecuting the Second Civil War.

The Death of a Monarch

On 20 January 1649, Charles was brought before a specially constituted High Court of Justice in Westminster Hall. He refused to recognize the legality of the court on the grounds that the king was appointed by God so no jurisdiction on earth could try him. Claiming that he stood for the liberty of the people of England he refused to plead. The court did not agree. On 27 January 1649, he was sentenced to death as a tyrant, traitor, murderer and public enemy.

Charles was beheaded on a scaffold in front of the Banqueting House in Whitehall on 30 January 1649. He died claiming to be a 'martyr for the people'. A week later he was buried in Windsor.

Following the execution of Charles I, a republic called the Commonwealth of England was declared, in which Britain was ruled by Parliament and the

RIGHT *Charles I was put on trial for high treason and 'other high crimes against the realm of England'. He was tried by 68 members of Parliament. The other 67 MPs did not turn up.*

THE EXECUTION OF A KING

After the First Civil War, the parliamentarians accepted the fact that Charles I was still entitled to be king, albeit with limited powers. However, Charles could not leave well alone. His actions provoked a Second Civil War which resulted in the shedding of innocent blood. Consequently the House of Commons passed an Act of Parliament that made it possible to put Charles on trial.

The idea of trying a king was a novel one. Previous monarchs had been deposed but had never been brought to trial. The Act established the High Court of Justice which consisted of 135 commissioners – although only about half actually sat in judgment. The prosecution was led by solicitor-general John Cooke. Fearing assassination the president of the court, John Bradshaw, wore a bullet-proof hat.

Charles' trial, on charges of high treason and other high crimes, began on 20 January 1649. Because the year began in March at that time,

ABOVE *Charles was executed on a scaffold erected outside the Banqueting Hall in Whitehall on 30 January 1649.*

the date is often recorded as 1648. Charles refused to enter a plea on the grounds that no court had jurisdiction over a monarch. He claimed that his own authority to rule had been given to him by God when he was crowned and anointed, while the court's authority resided merely in the force of arms. The court argued that no man was above the law.

When Cooke read the indictment, Charles I tried to stop him by poking at him with his cane. The ornate silver tip of the cane fell off and Cooke refused to pick it up. After a long pause, Charles stooped to retrieve it. This is considered an important moment, because it symbolized the divine monarch bowing before human law. Over the following week, Charles was given the opportunity to plead three times. Each time he refused. At that time a refusal to plead was normally taken as an admission of guilt. However, the court heard witnesses and appeared to do its best to give Charles a fair hearing. But on 29 January 1649 Charles' death warrant was signed by 59 of the commissioners.

The execution was due to take place early in the morning of 30 January 1649, although it was delayed until later in the day. It had been decided that no monarch should be able to follow Charles. So an ordinance making it treason to proclaim a successor was rushed through Parliament.

Charles was moved from St James's Palace to the Palace of Whitehall, where he prayed calmly throughout the morning. He was then brought to the scaffold that had been erected in front of the Banqueting House. He famously wore two shirts so that he would not shiver in the cold and so give an appearance of fear or weakness. After a last prayer, he put his head on the block and said, 'We shall go from a corruptible to an incorruptible crown, where no disturbance can be'. He then signalled the executioner who beheaded him with one clean stroke.

It was common practice for the head of a traitor to be held up and exhibited to the crowd with the words 'Behold the head of a traitor'. Although Charles' head was exhibited, these words do not seem to have been used. In an unprecedented gesture, Oliver Cromwell allowed Charles' head to be sewn back on to his body so that the family could pay its respects. On the night of 7 February 1649, Charles' body was taken to St George's Chapel in Windsor Castle and quietly placed in Henry VIII's vault.

ABOVE *A covenanter is arrested in Edinburgh. The covenanters had fought against Charles I in the Bishops' War, then supported him in the Civil War, but they were persecuted during the Restoration.*

increasingly tyrannical Oliver Cromwell, who became lord protector in 1653. When he died in 1658 he was replaced by his son Richard Cromwell, but he was not a strong enough character to unite the increasingly divided nation. The New Model Army and Parliament were unable to agree on a form of government. By excluding the army the Puritans and the royalists managed to agree to the restoration of the crown in 1660.

Under the agreement the powers of Parliament, which had been eroded during the Commonwealth, would be restored, along with those of the monarchy. Richard Cromwell then went into exile in France. He returned to England in 1680 and lived in seclusion in Cheshunt until his death in 1712 at the age of 86.

The Restoration

After Richard Cromwell's abdication, the eldest surviving son of Charles I was invited to take the throne in 1660. Born on 29 May 1630, Charles II (r.1660–85) was 12 years old when the Civil War broke out. Two years later he was appointed nominal commander-in-chief in western England. Following the parliamentary victory he escaped to France. He was in the Netherlands when, in 1649, he learnt of his father's execution.

In 1650, Charles put aside his Catholic sympathies and did a deal with the Scottish covenanters, who proclaimed him king. He then invaded England at the head of a Scottish army, but he was defeated by Cromwell at the Battle of Worcester in 1651. After 40 days on the run he returned to France but he moved on to Spain after Cromwell sought an alliance with the French. Although he was nominally king of England, Ireland and Scotland, he was shunned by the other European monarchs.

But Charles' fortunes changed in 1659, when Major-General John Lambert dissolved Parliament by force and a new military regime seized power. George Monck, one of Cromwell's leading generals, refused to recognize the new regime and led an army against Lambert.

OLIVER CROMWELL

Oliver Cromwell was born in Huntingdon on 25 April 1599, to a family of Protestants who had benefited from Henry VIII's dissolution of the monasteries. His father was a member of Parliament and a justice of the peace. After studying at Sidney Sussex College, Cambridge and Lincoln's Inn, Cromwell became MP for Huntingdon in the parliament of 1628–9. In the 1630s he experienced a religious crisis and became convinced that after being 'the chief of sinners' he had become one of God's chosen. He began to make his name as a radical Puritan when, in 1640, he was elected to represent Cambridge, first in the Short Parliament and then in the Long Parliament.

Although Cromwell lacked military experience when the Civil War broke out in 1642, he created a superb force of cavalry known as the 'Ironsides'. In just three years, he rose from the rank of captain to lieutenant-general. In 1644, he convinced Parliament of the need to establish a professional army, the New Model Army, which won a decisive victory over the king's forces at Naseby in 1645. Charles' alliance with the Scots, and the events of the Second Civil War, convinced Cromwell that the king must be brought to justice. He was a prime mover behind the trial and execution of Charles I in 1649.

After Charles' execution, Cromwell won conservative support for the new republic by suppressing radical elements in the army. He became army commander and lord lieutenant of Ireland, where he crushed resistance by massacring the garrisons at Drogheda and Wexford in 1649. Cromwell went on to defeat the supporters of the king's son Charles II at Dunbar in 1650 and Worcester in 1651, effectively ending royalist resistance. He then became convinced that the remaining rump of the Long Parliament was corrupt and on 20 April 1653 he marched into the house and dissolved it by force. He convened a hand-picked legislative body known as Barebones Parliament. When Cromwell was offered the crown he declined it. However, he assumed most of the powers of a monarch when he became lord protector on 16 December 1653. He then imposed his will on England by closing the theatres, stripping churches of their ornamentation and laying down strict laws for Sunday observance. Cromwell's strict Puritanism made him unpopular. However, he opposed severe punishments for minor crimes and capital punishment was restricted to murder, treason and rebellion. He also allowed the Jews, who had been expelled by Edward I in 1290, back into England.

ABOVE *Oliver Cromwell refused the crown, but appointed himself lord protector, a position that had similar powers.*

Cromwell's foreign policy was based on the expansion of English trade rather than the promotion of Protestantism. He ended the war with Portugal in 1653 and Holland in 1654. Trade rivalry precipitated England's war with Spain in 1654, but Cromwell joined forces with the French. The Commonwealth gained Jamaica in 1655 and Dunkirk in 1658, following the Battle of the Dunes.

The lord protector died on 3 September 1658 in London and was secretly interred in Westminster Abbey on 10 November, 13 days before his state funeral. After the Restoration his body was dug up and hanged at Tyburn like a common criminal. His head was then stuck on a pole on top of Westminster Hall, where it remained until the end of Charles II's reign.

A new parliament then invited Charles to reclaim his throne. Monck had already persuaded Charles to move from Catholic Spain to the

ABOVE *John Lambert was a leading parliamentary general during the Civil War and the principal architect of Cromwell's Protectorate.*

Protestant Netherlands. It was here, on 4 April 1660, that he issued the Declaration of Breda. Among other things, the proclamation offered a general pardon to his father's enemies, a free parliament and religious tolerance. The details were to be worked out by the so-called Convention Parliament. By this time, most Englishmen were tired of war and favoured the return of a stable, legitimate monarch. Charles landed in Dover on 25 May and was in London in time to celebrate his 30th birthday.

The pardon did not extend to those who had signed Charles I's death warrant. Ten were publicly hanged, drawn and quartered. Those who had already died were attainted for treason and their property was confiscated.

Twenty escaped to America or the Continent, although three were tracked down and extradited. Otherwise the new king pursued a policy of political tolerance and liberty. The 1679 *Habeas Corpus* Act was passed into law under Charles. His desire for religious tolerance led him to issue the Royal Declaration of Indulgence in 1672, which removed all laws against Roman Catholics and Nonconformists. However, Parliament forced him to retract the document.

Nevertheless, his popularity was assured when he reopened the theatres and other public entertainments that had been banned under the Puritans. He was known as the 'Merry Monarch' for his numerous love affairs with women – most famously with Nell Gwyn, the Drury Lane orange-seller – and 'Old Rowley' after his favourite stallion. Charles was such a great fan of horse-racing that he made the Newmarket meeting a biannual event.

Five years after Charles came to the throne, the plague returned to England. In the following year, 1666, the Great Fire of London raged through the city, which led to substantial rebuilding. During the Commonwealth, Britain had won the First Anglo-Dutch War of 1652–4, which was provoked by England's maritime trade monopoly.

Between 1665 and 1667, England undertook a Second Anglo-Dutch War, a squabble about Dutch possessions in Africa and North America. But Charles lost this war.

In 1670, Charles signed the Treaty of Dover with Louis XIV of France (1643–1715). He undertook to convert to Catholicism and support the French against the Dutch in what became the Third Anglo-Dutch War of 1672–4. In return, Charles received £160,000 a year from France, which allowed him some financial freedom from Parliament.

Then in 1677 Charles arranged the marriage of his niece Mary, daughter of his brother James, to the Protestant William of Orange. One of Charles' motives was to re-establish his Protestant credentials. Although Charles had a number of illegitimate children with various mistresses, his wife Catherine of Braganza was barren. Consequently his Catholic brother James became his heir, although the Exclusion Bill was an attempt to stop this happening. This bill, and his collusion with France against the Netherlands, brought Charles into conflict with Parliament. So he dissolved it in 1681, ruling alone until his death in 1685.

However, politics had moved into a new age with the establishment of the two-party system. The names of the two parties — the Tories and the Whigs — were originally terms of contempt. Tory meant an Irish outlaw — or *tóraidhe;* Whig was the name given to the country bumpkins,

LEFT *Louis XIV of France signed the Treaty of Dover with Charles II, giving him money for his support. In a secret clause, Charles promised to become a Catholic.*

or 'whiggamores', from Scotland who were part of the covenanters' force that marched on Edinburgh in 1648.

Charles' reign also saw the rise of trade and colonization in India and the East Indies. Then Britain captured New Amsterdam, later New York, from the Dutch in 1664. The passage of a series of Navigation Acts, restricting trade to British ships, further secured Britain's future as a sea power. Charles II also founded the Royal Society in 1660, which promoted the development of science. He died on 6 February 1685, having formally converted to Catholicism on his deathbed.

LEFT *Nell Gwyn was the most famous of Charles II's many mistresses. She was popular with the people because she was a Protestant.*

137

The Glorious Revolution

Charles II was succeeded by James II of England (r.1685–8) who was also James VII of Scotland. Born on 14 October 1633 and created duke of York in the following year, James saw service in the Civil War. He was captured in Oxford when the city fell in June 1646, but escaped to the Netherlands in April 1648. Early in the following year, he joined his mother in France. Joining the French army in April 1652, he distinguished himself as a soldier. However, when his brother Charles concluded an alliance with Spain in 1656, he switched his allegiance. He then commanded the right wing of the Spanish army against the French at the Battle of the Dunes, near Dunkirk, in June 1658.

James returned to England after the Restoration. He was the Lord High Admiral from 1660 to 1673, seeing action in the Second and Third Anglo-Dutch Wars. The taking of New Amsterdam had been his doing – it was renamed New York in his honour.

In 1660, James married Anne Hyde, daughter of Charles II's chief minister – they had two surviving children, Mary II and Anne. In 1669 James converted to Catholicism, although Charles insisted that he continue raising his daughters as Protestant. James' Catholicism led Parliament to pass the Test Act of 1673, which restricted public office to those who receive the sacraments of the Church of England. As a consequence, James was removed from the office of lord high admiral. James caused further offence to the Protestants by marrying the Catholic Mary of Modena when his first wife died. By 1678, rumours of a 'Popish Plot' were circulating. The defrocked Anglican clergyman Titus Oates spread the story that the Jesuits planned to assassinate Charles II and put James on the throne. Oates was found to be lying and the panic died down. The fabrication did not impede James' accession to the throne on Charles' death in 1685.

Later in 1685 James faced a rebellion led by Charles II's illegitimate son, the duke of Monmouth. The rebellion was crushed in July at the Battle of Sedgemoor. Justice was swift. The infamous lord chief justice, Judge Jeffreys, held a series of trials known as the 'Bloody Assizes'. Some 320 rebels were hanged while a further 800 were transported to Barbados. Hundreds more were fined or flogged – if they did not die in prison. Monmouth himself was messily beheaded. It took between five and eight strokes to sever his head.

James' attempts to extend civic equality to Roman Catholic and Protestant dissenters led him into conflict

BELOW *The Battle of the Dunes in 1658 – the duke of York, later James II, commanded the right wing of the Spanish army.*

THE WARMING-PAN FICTION

The birth of James II's son, James Francis Edward, in 1688 was highly controversial. His mother, Mary of Modena, had previously given birth to five children, the last in 1683, but none of them had survived infancy. This was a great relief to many observers, because it was widely feared that James II wanted to re-establish Roman Catholicism as the state religion. A male heir would supplant James' Protestant half-sisters, Princess Mary of Orange and Princess Anne of Denmark, in the succession.

Protestants began to question the child's legitimacy from the moment the queen's pregnancy was announced in November 1687. Those who were obliged to be present during the queen's lying-in stood with their backs to her bed, so that they could not be called upon to provide eyewitness testimony. When the queen gave birth to a healthy son, the rumour circulated that the real baby had died and a substitute had been smuggled into her bed in a warming pan. James II tried in vain to discredit the 'warming-pan fiction' by publishing the depositions of over seventy witnesses, but no one was prepared to believe the evidence.

ABOVE *James II was a Catholic. His second wife was a Catholic. When she gave birth to a Catholic heir, Protestant England decided enough was enough.*

LEFT *James' son by Mary of Modena grew up to be James Edward Stuart, the Old Pretender, father of Bonnie Prince Charlie.*

with Parliament when it was recalled in 1685. So James prorogued Parliament and ruled alone. He also attempted to promote Catholicism by appointing Catholics to military, political and academic posts. In 1687, he issued the Declaration of Indulgence, which called for complete religious toleration. Anglican clergy were instructed to read it from their pulpits.

In June 1688 Mary of Modena gave birth to a son, James Francis Edward. A Catholic succession now seemed inevitable so a group of six prominent politicians and one bishop issued an invitation to the Protestant William of

Orange, husband of James' eldest daughter Mary. In November, William landed with an army at Brixham in Devon. Deserted by the army and the navy, whom he had completely alienated – including his best general John Churchill, the future duke of Marlborough – James lost his nerve and fled abroad. In February 1689, Parliament declared that James' flight constituted an abdication and William and Mary were crowned as joint monarchs in what was known as the Glorious Revolution. A Bill of Rights was passed which gave the succession to Mary's sister Anne if William and Mary had no children. It also barred Roman Catholics from the throne, abolished the Crown's power to suspend laws and declared a standing army illegal in times of peace.

However, James was determined to recover the throne. In March 1689, he landed in Ireland where a parliament in Dublin acknowledged him as king. James raised an army with French support, but he was defeated by William of Orange at the Battle of the Boyne in July 1690. With nowhere to turn he returned to France. The Treaty of Rijswijk between England and France in 1697 put an end to any further hopes and James died in exile in Saint-Germain-en-Laye in France on 16 September 1701.

William and Mary

William III of Orange was born in The Hague on 4 November 1650. His father, who died eight days before his birth, was William II of Orange (r.1647–50) and his mother was Mary Stuart, the daughter of Charles I. Although the Orange family was the most powerful in the Netherlands, its members were not hereditary sovereigns. In fact, the House of Orange was specifically excluded from office by the Act of Seclusion of 1654. Then in 1672 Louis XIV of France invaded the United Provinces of the Netherlands during the Third Anglo-Dutch war. The Dutch invited William to be their 'stadtholder', or chief magistrate, thereby making him their military commander.

It was a good move. He succeeded in driving the French out of the Netherlands and became a champion of Protestantism in Europe.

In 1677 William married his cousin Mary, the eldest daughter of James, duke of York, heir to the English throne. William hoped that this union would cement an Anglo-Dutch alliance against the expansionist hopes of the French. But things changed after James became king and Mary of Modena had a son. English Protestants feared that England would turn Catholic again so they made secret overtures to William. When William brought his army to England in November 1688 James found himself without support, so he was forced to flee to France.

Early in 1689, Parliament formally offered William and Mary the throne as joint monarchs. It also presented them with a Declaration of Rights, which later became a Bill of Rights. This outlined grievances against James, limited the power of the monarchy and affirmed important rights relating to the powers of Parliament – making William and Mary England's first constitutional monarchs. They were crowned king and queen of England on 21 April, and William was offered the crown of Scotland, as William II, later that month. He was, of course, William III in England.

James landed in Ireland in March 1689, accompanied by a number of French troops. Ireland was then predominantly Catholic, so he enjoyed widespread support. The Jacobites in Scotland also rose up to support James. William took an army to Ireland and defeated James at the Battle of the Boyne in July 1690. He then became William I of Ireland.

BELOW *In the Popish Plot, Titus Oates claimed that a Catholic conspiracy was afoot. He was convicted of perjury, pilloried, flogged and imprisoned.*

TITUS OATES

In the following year, William offered to pardon the Highland clans for their part in the Jacobite risings. But they had to take the oath of allegiance before 1 January 1692 – in front of a magistrate. Although widespread refusals were expected, most chiefs took the oath. However, Alexander MacDonald of Glencoe postponed his submission until 31 December 1691, only to find that there was no magistrate at Fort William to receive it. A punishment order was issued and over a hundred soldiers descended on the clan. The troops were mainly Campbells, who were serving with the Argyll regiment. To make matters worse, they had been peacefully billeted with the MacDonalds for over a week. During the Massacre of Glencoe the chief, 33 men, two women and two children were slaughtered. William ordered an investigation, but no further action was taken until the Scottish parliament demanded a public enquiry in 1695. The massacre was blamed on

Sir John Dalrymple, earl of Stair, who was dismissed. However, to this day the old Clachaig Inn at Glencoe carries a sign on its door which bears the words 'No Campbells'.

But Louis XIV of France was William's main concern. In 1689 William had made Britain part of the Grand Alliance – a coalition of European powers formed to oppose France. As a result the first eight years of William's reign were taken up with fighting, first in Ireland and then on the Continent. The national debt he had built up was secured by William Paterson, a Scottish merchant. Paterson established the Bank of England in 1694 and the Bank of Scotland in the following year. The fighting came to an end when Louis XIV signed the Treaty of Rijswijk in 1697. Under its terms Louis surrendered much of the territory he had won and recognized William as England's king. James II's hopes for a restoration were thus dashed.

ABOVE *William III aimed to put an end to the Stuart cause at the Battle of the Boyne in July 1690, and by pardoning the Scottish Jacobites the following year.*

Mary had died of smallpox in 1694 leaving William to rule alone. He died in a hunting accident on 8 March 1702, when his horse tripped over a molehill and threw him. This gave rise to the Jacobite toast, 'To the little gentleman in black velvet'. At the time of his death William was constructing a new Grand Alliance against France.

William and Mary had no children and it is likely that their marriage was celibate. As a youth Mary had shared girlfriends with her sister Anne, while William was more interested in men than women. After William's death, Mary's sister succeeded to the throne as Queen Anne (r.1702–14), the last of the Stuart monarchs.

Born on 6 February 1665, Anne was the second daughter of the Catholic James, duke of York, but was raised a Protestant under the guidance of her uncle Charles II. Her marriage to George, prince of Denmark in 1683 was devoted, if politically uneventful. Between 1683 and 1700 she fell pregnant 18 times, but only five children were born alive. One child, William, outlived infancy, but he did not survive long enough to inherit the throne.

Anne's early favourite was Sarah Jennings Churchill, a childhood companion and lady of the bedchamber. It was Sarah who persuaded Anne to support her brother-in-law William of Orange when he overthrew her father James II in 1688. James' downfall led to Anne's accession in 1702. Almost the whole of her reign was taken up by the War of the Spanish Succession (1701–14), in which a coalition of European powers fought to prevent the French from taking over the throne of Spain. It was at this time that Sarah Churchill's husband, the duke of Marlborough, won his famous victories at Blenheim, Ramillies, Oudenarde and Malplaquet. The conflict also included Queen Anne's War, in North America, which won for Britain Nova Scotia, Newfoundland and Hudson Bay.

There was still a chance that the Scots might choose a separate monarch so on 1 May 1707 Anne presided over the Act of

Union. Scotland and England then became a single country with a single parliament at Westminster. A common flag and currency were created, although Scotland would keep its own established Church and systems of law and education.

Anne's reign was marked by the development of the two-party system, in which Whigs and Tories competed for power. The duke of Marlborough was a Whig sympathizer so Sarah Churchill put Anne under pressure to promote Whigs in her ministry. But the queen resisted and eventually dismissed the overbearing couple. Sarah's successor as Anne's favourite, Abigail Masham, was a cousin of the Tory Robert Harley, who later became earl of Oxford. Abigail's position allowed Harley to influence the queen. But in 1708 Harley also lost favour and Anne was forced to admit the Whigs into her administration again. Then in 1710 there was a major shift to the Tories, which lasted until her death.

During Anne's reign some disaffected

THE BILL OF RIGHTS

Under the Bill of Rights of 1689, Englishmen were awarded a number of immutable civil and political rights. Perhaps more importantly for the time, the Bill set strict limits on the royal family's legal prerogatives. Some of the rights contained in the Bill were:

- Freedom from royal interference with the law – sovereigns were forbidden to establish their own courts or to act as judges.
- Freedom from taxation by the sovereign without the agreement of Parliament.
- Freedom to petition the monarch.
- Freedom from a peacetime standing army without the agreement of Parliament.
- Freedom for Protestants to bear arms for their defence, suitable to their class status and as allowed by law.
- Freedom to elect members of Parliament without interference from the sovereign.
- Freedom of speech in Parliament – proceedings in Parliament are not to be questioned in the courts or in any place outside Parliament itself. This is the basis of modern parliamentary privilege.
- Freedom from cruel and unusual punishments and excessive bail.
- Freedom from fines and forfeitures without trial.

The sovereign was also required to summon Parliament frequently. This clause was reinforced by the Triennial Act of 1694. Certain acts of James II were specifically named and declared illegal and the flight of James from England was deemed to amount to abdication of the throne. William and Mary were to be his successors. In future Roman Catholics could not be king or queen of England since 'it hath been found by experience that it is inconsistent with the safety and welfare of this protestant kingdom to be governed by a papist prince'. The sovereign was required to swear a coronation oath to maintain the Protestant religion. After William and Mary, the succession should pass to the heirs of Mary, then to Mary's sister Princess Anne of Denmark and her heirs, then to any heirs of William by a later marriage.

Tories plotted the return of her exiled Catholic half-brother, James Francis Stuart, the Old Pretender, son of James II. However, under the 1713 Treaty of Utrecht France recognized the superiority of Anne's title over that of James Stuart. In any event, there was little call for the return of a Catholic king.

LEFT *Queen Anne was the daughter of James II and sister of Queen Mary. Allegations were made about her sexuality.*

CHAPTER SEVEN

VII

THE HANOVERIANS

THE HANOVERIANS

George I (1714–27)

George II (1727–60)

George III (1760–1820)

George IV (1820–30)

William IV (1830–7)

Dates show reign of monarch

LEFT *Sir Robert Walpole, earl of Orford, was generally regarded as Britain's first prime minister, coming to power under George I.*

The German Kings

After the death of Queen Anne in 1714 there was to be no return to the Stuart line. James Francis Stuart, the 'Old Pretender', and his son Charles Edward Stuart (Bonnie Prince Charlie), the 'Young Pretender', continued to push the Jacobite cause. But Parliament was determined to ensure that a Catholic would never again ascend the throne. When the duke of Gloucester, the last of Anne's seventeen children, died in 1701, the legal framework was put in place.

Under the Act of Settlement of 1701 the English throne would pass to Sophia, the electress of Hanover, if the reigning monarch William III and his heir Anne died

BELOW Bonnie Prince Charlie – Charles Edward Stuart – was the grandson of James II and tried to regain the British throne for the Stuarts.

without issue. Sophia was the granddaughter of James VI of Scotland, I of England, and niece of Charles I. At least fifty Catholics had a stronger claim to the throne than Sophia, but she was a Protestant. As it was, Sophia did not succeed. She died a few months before Anne, so her son George became king in August 1714.

George I (r. 1714–27) was born in Hanover, Germany on 28 May 1660. He was the eldest son of the duke of Brunswick-Lüneburg. In 1682, George married his cousin Sophia Dorothea of Celle and they had two children. But in 1694 he accused her of infidelity with a Swedish count, who was then murdered. George divorced his wife and imprisoned her in the castle of Ahlden, where she remained until her death in 1726.

George became the elector of Hanover on the death of his father in 1698. The War of the Spanish Succession began shortly afterwards and George fought alongside the English with distinction in the battle against the French. Whig politicians began to court him, while many Tories remained loyal to James

RIGHT Sophia, the electress of Hanover, would have become queen of England if she had not died a few months before Queen Anne.

FAR RIGHT With Sophia already dead by the time the throne became vacant, her son George, the elector of Hanover, took the crown as George I.

THE ACT OF SETTLEMENT

The 1701 Act of Settlement ensured that the throne would pass to the Electress Sophia of Hanover – granddaughter of James VI of Scotland, I of England, and niece of Charles I – and on to her Protestant descendants. The act barred those who were Roman Catholic – and those who married a Roman Catholic – from ascending the throne. Eight further provisions of the act would come into effect after the deaths of William of Orange and Queen Anne. These were:

- The monarch 'shall join in communion with the Church of England'. This prevented dissenters as well as Roman Catholics from taking the throne. Religion had been a major political problem in England for nearly 200 years. It had been the cause of the English Civil War as well as the Glorious Revolution of 1688.

- If a person not native to England comes to the throne, England will not wage war for 'any dominions or territories which do not belong to the crown of England, without the consent of Parliament'. This meant that England would not go to war for the interests of Hanover.

- No monarch may leave 'the dominions of England, Scotland, or Ireland', without the consent of Parliament. This provision was repealed in 1716 at the request of George I. As elector of Hanover and duke of Brunswick-Lüneburg he often needed to visit Hanover.

- All government matters within the jurisdiction of the Privy Council were to be transacted by the Privy Council, and all Privy Council resolutions were to be signed by those who advised and consented to them. Parliament wanted to know who was deciding policies. However, this clause was repealed early in Queen Anne's reign, because many privy councillors ceased to offer advice – some stopped attending meetings altogether.

- No foreigner, even if naturalized (unless they were born of English parents), shall be allowed to be a privy councillor or a member of either house of Parliament, or hold 'any office or place of trust, either civil or military, or to have any grant of lands, tenements or hereditaments from the crown, to himself or to any other or others in trust for him'. This has been modified by subsequent nationality laws.

- No person who has an office under the monarch, or receives a pension from the crown, can be a member of Parliament. MPs were not allowed to resign from Parliament but they could make themselves ineligible by serving the Crown in a low-salary capacity, such as the wardenship of the Chiltern Hundreds.

- Judges' commissions are only valid *quamdiu se bene gesserint* – that is, 'during good behaviour'. This means that if judges do not behave themselves they can be removed by Parliament. It effectively makes them independent of the monarch's influence and ensures almost complete judicial independence.

- No pardon by the monarch can save someone from being impeached by the House of Commons.

The Act of Settlement deliberately passed over the hereditary rights of the Stuarts, who continued to press their cause. The handing of the crown to the Hanoverians was purely statutory and the House of Brunswick has no hereditary right to the throne. In 1910 it was estimated that over a thousand descendants of Charles I had precedence over Queen Victoria, her son Edward VII, her grandson George V and her great-grandson Edward VIII.

THE JACOBITES

ABOVE *The Jacobite rising of 1715 was led by John Erskine, the earl of Mar, but his forces failed to win a decisive victory at Sheriffmuir despite outnumbering Hanoverian troops by two to one.*

The Jacobites were supporters of the exiled Stuart dynasty. They held court in France and Italy from 1688 to 1745 and presented a feasible alternative government. Many Tories became sympathetic to the Jacobites when the Whigs came to power in 1714. In all, there were five attempts to restore the Stuart line.

In 1689, supported by French troops and the Irish parliament, James II landed in Ireland. His attempt to reverse the Glorious Revolution foundered at the Battle of the Boyne on 1 July 1690, when he lost to an army under the personal command of William. Then James Francis Stuart, the 'Old Pretender' – son of James II – returned with a French invasion fleet in 1708, only to be met in the Firth of Forth by the Royal Navy. The French commander refused to put James ashore and the uprising foundered.

The third attempt came in 1715 when the earl of Mar persuaded the Scottish clans in the northeast to come to the support of 'James III and VIII', as the Old Pretender was known. Other Scots, who were opposed to the union with England, also rallied to his cause and a Catholic rebellion broke out in Lancashire. However, Mar failed to win an overwhelming victory at the Battle of Sheriffmuir on 13 November. The rebellion had run out of steam by the time the Old Pretender arrived in December. He promptly fled back to France with the leaders of the uprising.

James then mustered another invasion fleet in Spain, but most of it had been destroyed by a storm before it set sail. A small force arrived in northwest Scotland in June 1719, but it was scattered at the Battle of Glenshiel. A new French invasion plan collapsed again in 1744.

In 1745 came the fifth and last attempt to restore the Stuart line. This time the Old Pretender's son, Charles Edward Stuart – known as 'Bonnie Prince Charlie' – arrived alone. Charles commanded fewer Scottish Jacobites than his father had before him but the Hanoverians were short of men. The War of the Austrian Succession had drained Scotland of troops. A quick victory at Prestonpans on 21 September made Charles master of Scotland. However, he was not content to dissolve the Union and rule north of the border – he claimed the throne of Great Britain. His Scottish army marched south as far as Derby but when the English did not rise up in his support they turned north again. After another victory at Falkirk on 17 January 1746, Charles retreated into the Highlands.

On 16 April the Jacobite army was crushed by the king's second son, William Augustus, duke of Cumberland, at the battle of Culloden. Cumberland's men were using cannon, flintlocks and the latest Swedish rapid-fire techniques from the Continent. Some 80 of the rebels were executed and 1,000 more were tracked down and killed in the harsh repression that followed. With a price of £30,000 on his head Bonnie Prince Charlie evaded capture for six months in the Western Isles. In September 1746 he escaped back to France, then Florence. He finally died in Rome on 31 January 1788.

ABOVE RIGHT *The defeated Jacobites return home after the 1745 rebellion. All hope of putting the Stuarts back on the throne was gone.*

Stuart. But when Queen Anne died the Whigs seized control and put George I on the throne. In Scotland the Stuarts were still popular and Jacobite risings had to be put down in 1715 and 1719. Even in England George was far from popular, but he was regarded as the lesser of two evils.

The king's unpopularity increased when it emerged that he had treated his wife badly. He also invited ridicule when he arrived in England with his two mistresses – one thin and tall, the other short and fat. They were variously described as 'the hop-pole and the elephant' or 'the maypole and the Elephant and Castle'.

George was 54 years old when he came to the throne. It is said that he never took the trouble to learn English but instead communicated with his ministers in French. He spent more time in Hanover than in England, leaving the business of government to a Whig oligarchy that ruled England for the next 50 years. Their first leader was Sir Robert Walpole. In 1715, Walpole became first lord of the treasury and chancellor of the exchequer. After he resigned in 1717, he curried favour with Caroline of Ansbach, princess of Wales, who help him maintain power when her husband George II (r.1727–60) came to power.

Although Walpole had speculated on the South Sea Company, like most people around him, he avoided the scandal surrounding its collapse. In April 1721 he returned to the Government as first lord of the treasury and chancellor of the exchequer. As the leading figure in the Government he effectively became prime minister, although the term was not used at the time. He remained in this position of dominance until 1742. The king's credibility had been damaged by the South Sea Bubble fiasco but Walpole used his parliamentary influence to save

him from disgrace. In return, George gave Walpole and his Whig supporters a free hand in government.

George I died in Osnabruck on 11 June 1727 and was succeeded by his son George II. His daughter Sophia Dorothea (1687–1757) married King Frederick William I of Prussia (r.1713–40) in 1706 and was the mother of Frederick the Great (r.1740–86).

George II (r.1727–60) was born on 10 November 1683 in Hanover, where he grew up. In 1705 he married Princess Caroline of Brandenburg-Ansbach, and they had nine children. When his father, George I, succeeded

ABOVE *George II lacked self-confidence and depended heavily on his ministers, particularly Sir Robert Walpole.*

LEFT *Caroline of Brandenburg-Ansbach was George II's wife. George was devoted to her and she gave him nine children.*

to the British throne in 1714 George was created prince of Wales. But father and son detested each other and the prince's London residence, Leicester House, became a rival court and the focus for a dissident Whig group which included Robert Walpole, then out of favour. Walpole encouraged a reconciliation between the prince and his father, which led to Walpole's return to George I's administration. This temporarily lost him the prince's favour,

THE SOUTH SEA BUBBLE

The South Sea Company was founded by the lord treasurer, Robert Harley in 1711. In return for a slave-trading monopoly in Spanish South America it was hoped that the company would be able to fund the War of the Spanish Succession (1701–14). The company's fate depended on the treaty that followed the war but its stock, which guaranteed an interest rate of six per cent, sold well.

However, the Treaty of Utrecht (1713) severely limited the slave trade. Nevertheless, the company did well on its first voyage in 1717 and in the following year George I became its governor. Confidence soared and the company was soon paying investors 100 per cent interest.

So inflated was the paper value of the company that in 1720 it proposed taking over the national debt. The share price stood at just over £100 in January of that year but it had rocketed to more than £1,000 by August. In September the market collapsed and by December the shares were back

ABOVE *A satire from a 1721 edition of* The Weekly Journal and British Gazeteer, *on Robert Knight, the cashier of the South Sea Company.*

down to £124, dragging government and other stock down with them. Many investors were ruined. A House of Commons enquiry revealed that ministers had taken bribes. The directors were disgraced. Most of the rights were sold to the Spanish government in 1750, although the company itself survived until 1853.

but Walpole maintained his friendship with the prince's wife, Princess Caroline, who kept him in office when her husband succeeded to the throne. Queen Caroline died in 1737 and George did not marry again.

Walpole secured his position with George II by getting Parliament to grant him a Civil List of £800,000 – considerably more than previous monarchs had received. In 1735, George made Walpole a gift of 10 Downing Street, now the permanent London residence of the British prime minister. Like his father George II liked to spend much of his time in Hanover, which allowed Walpole to build up his dominant position in Parliament. In return, Walpole ensured that George had the backing of the many influential Tories who had previously supported Charles Edward Stuart's claim to the throne. Consequently, no senior politician deserted the Hanoverian cause during the Jacobite Rebellion of 1745 – despite the fact that Walpole was forced to resign in 1742. He died three years later.

George II quickly found another mentor in John Carteret, later Earl Granville, who supported George's vigorous pursuit of the War of the Austrian Succession (1740–8), prompting accusations that he was subordinating English interests to those of George's German possessions. In 1743, George led his troops into battle against the French at Dettingen. He was the last reigning monarch to lead his soldiers in the field.

But during the last decade of his life George took little interest in politics. Instead he spent much of his time indulging his passion for opera. He was a patron of the German composer George Frideric Handel, who had moved to London in 1710. Britain's involvement in the Seven Years' War (1756–63) was largely overseen by William Pitt the Elder. The conflict witnessed the expansion of British dominance in India and Canada, following the military successes of Clive and Wolfe.

George died on 25 October 1760 and was the last king to be buried at Westminster. His son Frederick Louis, prince of Wales, had died before his father in 1751, so the crown passed to his grandson who became George III.

BELOW *William Pitt the Elder, seen here speaking in favour of war.*

RIGHT *George III was the first of the Hanoverian kings to have English as his first language. Consequently, he sought to meddle in politics.*

Farmer George

Born on 4 June 1738 in London, George III (r.1760–1820) was the son of Frederick Louis, prince of Wales and Augusta of Saxe-Gotha. He became heir to the throne when his father died in 1751 and he succeeded his grandfather George II in 1760. In 1761, he married Charlotte Sophia of Mecklenburg-

RIGHT *Charlotte Sophia of Mecklenburg-Strelitz was married to George III. They had fifteen children together.*

THE SEVEN YEARS' WAR

The Seven Years' War (1756–63) can be seen as the first global conflict. It arose out of the attempt of the Austrian Habsburgs to win back Silesia, which had been wrested from them by Frederick the Great of Prussia. Hanover and Great Britain sided with Prussia while France, Russia, Sweden and Saxony backed Austria. However, the conflict between Britain and France turned into a colonial struggle for India and North America, where the French and Indian War (1754–63) for the control of the Ohio Valley had broken out. The European war began in 1756 when Frederick the Great invaded Saxony as a pre-emptive strike on Austria's allies. Frederick's army succeeded in occupying Dresden. Then the Prussian forces defeated the Austrians at the Battle of Prague in 1757 but they had to retreat after the Battle of Kolin. Meanwhile the Hanoverian army led by George II's younger son, the duke of Cumberland, was heavily defeated by the French at the Battle of Hastenbach.

Still in 1757, the Swedish and the Russians attacked Prussia and Austria seized Silesia. Frederick then defeated a Franco-German army at Rossbach and an Austrian force at Leuthen, even though he was heavily outnumbered. Further away, victory in the Battle of Plassey made Clive of India the master of Bengal.

The French occupation of Hanover was short-lived. It ended when a joint British and Hanoverian army defeated a Franco-Austrian force at Krefeld in June 1758. Frederick II defeated the Russians at Zorndorg in August 1758 but the Russians turned the tables at Kunersdorf in the following August. The Prussians were then defeated by the Austrians at Hochkirck in October.

By contrast, the British were victorious on land, at sea and in the colonies. They defeated the French at the Battle of Minden on 1 August 1759 and in the naval Battle of Lagos, off the coast of Portugal, in the middle of the same

ABOVE *All the major European powers were involved in the Seven Years' War. Prussia emerged as winner on the Continent, while Britain gained ground in India and North America.*

month. In September James Wolfe captured Quebec from the French and on 20 November the British defeated the French in the naval Battle of Quiberon Bay, Brittany. The enemy fleet was on its way to invade Scotland.

Britain's success continued in 1760 when the French were defeated at the Battle of Wandiwash near Madras on 22 January. That was the end of French hopes in India. Frederick II ended the short occupation of Berlin by the Russians in October and he defeated the Austrians at Torgau on 3 November, although losses were heavy on both sides. In January of 1761 Britain triumphed again at Pondicherry in India and the Germans defeated the French at Villinghause in the following July.

Things changed when George II died because George III ended British aid to Prussia. But just when Prussia appeared to be doomed Elizabeth of Russia (r.1741–62) died and Peter III (r.1762) succeeded her. The new Tsar was a great admirer of Frederick II. Although he reigned for just four months he quickly moved to end the war between Prussia and Russia with the Treaty of St Petersburg, signed on 5 May 1762. The war now turned decisively in favour of Britain and Prussia. Frederick II defeated the Austrians at Burkersdorf on 21 July 1762 and Reichenbach on 16 August, regaining all of his lost territory.

Meanwhile the British captured Havana and Manila from the Spanish. Peace between Britain and France was restored by the Treaty of Paris on 10 February 1763. Britain returned Cuba and the Philippines to Spain while retaining the territory she had won from the French in North America and India. Then peace between Austria, Prussia and Saxony was restored by the Treaty of Hubertusberg on 15 February 1763, which confirmed Silesia as Prussian territory.

The Seven Years' War saw Britain established as the greatest colonial power in the world, with control over India and North America seemingly secured. Prussia emerged as the greatest power on the Continent and the dominant force inside Germany. The power of the Holy Roman Empire and Habsburg Austria had been reduced even further.

THE AMERICAN WAR OF INDEPENDENCE

The cost of the Anglo-French wars had made some people in Britain feel that the colonies should make a contribution to their own administration and defence. Taxation seemed to be the only solution but this policy quickly alienated the colonists. The Stamp Act of 1765, the first tax on internal trade, was denounced as a violation of the Englishman's traditional right to be taxed only through his elected representatives. It was repealed in 1766. However, in 1767 the new chancellor of the exchequer Charles Townshend introduced the Revenue Act which taxed imports. The colonists reacted by boycotting incoming goods. When Lord North came to power in 1770, he withdrew all import taxes, except those on tea. But the protests continued. In an incident known as the Boston Massacre, a small detachment of British troops opened fire after being set upon by a mob.

ABOVE *In the Boston Tea Party, colonists dumped tea into the harbour as a protest against the monopoly of the East India Company.*

Five people were killed. The soldiers were charged with murder and were given a civilian trial. However a successful defence was conducted by John Adams. Ironically, he was a leading revolutionary who went on to become the second president of the United States.

Then in 1773 Lord North tried to assist the ailing East India Company by introducing a Tea Act. This gave the company a monopoly on the sale of tea, thereby cutting out the American merchants. Colonial resistance came to a head with the incident of the Boston Tea Party of December 1773, when a bunch of colonists disguised as Mohawk Indians dumped £10,000 worth of tea into the harbour. The port was closed and the colonial charter of Massachusetts was altered, while the elected council was replaced with an appointed one. New England Puritans were further outraged by the Quebec Act of 1774, which recognized the right of the French citizens of Canada to practise Catholicism.

A Colonial Congress was called in 1774, at which the colonists sought to redress their grievances by diplomacy. Nevertheless, some revolutionaries began to arm. When British troops entered Lexington and Concord on 19 April 1775, in order to seize American military stores, fighting broke out with the local militia. In June a second Colonial Congress held in Philadelphia raised an army under the command of Virginia delegate George Washington and in August George III declared a state of rebellion. At that time, most Americans remained loyal to the British crown. But in January 1776 Tom Paine put the case for independence in the pamphlet *Common Sense*. It sold 500,000 copies. The Declaration of Independence quickly followed. It was signed on 4 July 1776.

Washington's army was largely unsuccessful until the end of 1776. But things suddenly changed at the beginning of the following year. The colonists scored stunning victories at Trenton and Princeton and the French rushed to join them. Spain joined the cause in 1779, followed by the Netherlands in 1780. In August 1781 a combined force of colonists and French troops, led by Washington and Count de Rochambeau, cornered the British at Yorktown. The end came on 19 October 1781, when the British General Cornwallis surrendered. Peace was concluded at the Treaty of Paris in 1782, with Britain recognizing the independence of the United States.

However, maritime conflicts and disputes over the Canadian border led to the War of 1812. Although the British took Washington, DC and burned public buildings including the White House, both sides grew tired of warfare. The Treaty of Ghent was signed on 24 December 1814, which returned the two countries to *status quo ante bellum* – that is, things as they were before the war. However, news of the peace treaty had not reached America by 8 January 1815 because General – later President – Andrew Jackson defeated the British at the Battle of New Orleans.

Strelitz. Their 50-year marriage produced 15 children.

George III was the first Hanoverian monarch to have English as his first language. Consequently he wanted to rule on his own terms, so he sought to wrest power back from the prime ministers who had taken over the government of the country during the reigns of his predecessors. Parliament did not depend on popular support because many MPs sat at the behest of individual patrons, so George found it relatively easy to replace the long-standing Whig ministry with a Tory administration. George chose the earl of Bute as his first chief minister, who ended the Seven Years' War. Together they sought to break the power of the Whigs.

But Bute was a poor choice because he isolated George from the other senior politicians. Effective government became almost impossible. Bute was also being vilified by the radical journalist John Wilkes, whose attacks forced his resignation in 1763. The Crown was still struggling with the financial consequences of the Seven Years' War so George turned to George Grenville for assistance. Grenville in his turn was savaged by Wilkes, who was eventually expelled from Parliament. He was also prosecuted for seditious libel and obscenity because of his parody of Alexander Pope's *Essay on Man,* which he called *Essay on Woman.*

Overseas trade expanded greatly under Grenville but the lucrative East India Company made no significant contribution to the exchequer. But it was Grenville's mishandling of colonial taxation that brought about his downfall – notably the Stamp Act of 1765. William Pitt returned to office in 1766 and joined George in repealing this hugely unpopular tax on the American colonists. When Pitt became ill he was replaced by

the duke of Grafton, but the duke could not maintain a government.

George then appointed Lord North as his first minister in 1770. Although North was an effective administrator, his government was dominated by disagreements with the American colonists over British attempts to levy taxes on them. In 1775 the inevitable American War of Independence began. George was determined to prolong the war until the rebels gave in, but the fight was over when Lord Cornwallis surrendered at Yorktown in 1781. After that, North was forced to resign.

In 1783, the Tory Lord North and the prominent Whig politician Charles James Fox formed a coalition government. George disliked Fox intensely so when his coalition put forward a plan to reform the East India Company he opposed it. It appeared that Fox's cronies would be the new company's commissioners. Posing as the guardian of the national interest, George forced the bill's defeat in Parliament, and the two resigned in 1783. In their place George appointed William Pitt the Younger, who was an inspired choice. During and after his administration George became very popular with the British people. Britain's war with France in 1793 further increased his standing. However, Pitt favoured the emancipation of the Catholics while George was vehemently opposed to the move, which forced Pitt to resign in 1801.

BELOW *The painter Joshua Reynolds was the first president of the Royal Academy of Arts, founded in 1768 under the patronage of George III.*

The loss of the American colonies and family quarrels put great strain on George's health. After serious bouts of illness in 1788, 1789 and 1801, now thought to be caused by the blood disease porphyria, he became permanently deranged in 1810. The prince of Wales – later George IV (r.1820–30) – became regent in 1811 after his father was declared insane. George remained ill until his death at Windsor Castle on 29 January 1820.

Britain had changed substantially during George's 59-year reign. First there was the Industrial Revolution, during which there was a dramatic

THE NAPOLEONIC WARS

Following the French Revolution of 1789, the rest of Europe was concerned that France might seek to export its revolution. Indeed, France declared war on Austria in 1792. Prussia, Britain and the other European nations joined a coalition against the French in 1793, but by 1797 Britain stood alone. However, a series of naval victories – notably the Battle of the Nile in 1798 and the Battle of Copenhagen in 1801 – left Britain in control of the seas, while the French dominated the Continent. This was recognized in the Treaty of Amiens in 1802 and the short-lived peace that followed.

But Napoleon Bonaparte was committed to the expansion of France. He seized power as first consul in 1799 and then became emperor in 1804. Intent on invading England, he was finally thwarted by Nelson's defeat of the combined French and Spanish fleets off Cape Trafalgar in 1805. Napoleon then resorted to economic warfare in an attempt to bankrupt what he called 'a nation of shopkeepers'. But the subject nations of Europe grew restive. Spain and Portugal revolted in 1808 and the British went to their aid in the Peninsular War (1808–13).

ABOVE *When Napoleon took power, he wrote to George III making peace. But Pitt the Younger was determined to continue the war.*

In 1812 Napoleon invaded Russia. Although he reached Moscow, his army was wiped out by the harsh Russian winter. He was forced to abdicate and was then exiled to the Italian island of Elba. However, while the victors were meeting to redraw the map of Europe at the Congress of Vienna in 1815, Napoleon escaped. Returning to France, where his troops rallied to him, he began his 'Hundred Days'. His final escapade ended in defeat when he met the superior forces of the duke of Wellington and the Prussian Marshal Blücher at the Battle of Waterloo.

Napoleon was finally exiled to the remote island of St Helena in the South Atlantic, where he died in 1821.

swing towards machine-based manufacturing. New roads and canals were built and the population more than doubled. There were many more mouths to feed, so agriculture needed to develop at the same pace as industry. Recognizing this need, George created a model farm at Windsor, earning himself the nickname 'Farmer George'. His other hobbies were making buttons and putting watches together and he had a flair for music, furniture and gardens.

Then in 1801 a new Act of Union was passed, which united Great Britain and Ireland into a single nation. This arrangement remained unchanged until the Government of Ireland Act of 1920. George III was the first king of this new United Kingdom.

George III also had a great influence on the world of art and literature. He founded the Royal Academy in 1768, with Sir Joshua Reynolds as its first president and he created an important library. His books were moved to the British Museum in 1823 and they are now in the British Library.

Victory in the French Revolutionary and Napoleonic Wars, under the leadership of the duke of Wellington, made Britain a formidable military power during George's reign. And Lord Nelson's victory at the battle of Trafalgar confirmed Britain's domination of the seas. The Atlantic slave trade was banned in 1807 while slavery ended in most of the British Empire in 1833.

A Pas de Deux or Love at first Sight.
How I'd love you all the day   If with me you'd fondly stray
Every Night we'd Kiss and Play Over the Hills and far away.

ABOVE *'Love at first sight' was a satire on Caroline of Brunswick's affair with Bartolomeo Pergami.*

The Extravagant Monarch

George III was succeeded by George IV, his eldest son, who had already served as regent since 1811. Like previous Hanoverians, George IV did not have a good relationship with his father, who had long regarded his extravagant lifestyle with contempt.

As prince of Wales George IV set up his own court at Carlton House, which became the hub of fashionable London society. He was also a patron of art and architecture and Regent's Street, Regent's Park and the Regency Style were named after him.

THE CATO STREET CONSPIRACY AND OTHER REPUBLICAN PLOTS

The spirit of revolution was not confined to the Americans and the French. London was rocked by the anti-Catholic Gordon Riots in 1780, which left the capital lawless for three days. Then the French spy François Henri de la Motte was hanged at Tyburn on 27 July 1781. He had been supplying the Americans, allies of the French, with British naval intelligence. Some said he had even threatened the king's life. After half an hour on the gibbet he was cut down and his head was severed and shown to the crowd. His heart was cut out and burnt and his body was scored with a knife as a symbolic form of quartering.

ABOVE *This is how the Cato Street Conspiracy was supposed to have turned out. Instead, the conspirators were arrested before they had fired the first shot.*

In 1792 there were rumours of a planned insurrection in London. The Loyal Lambeth Association drilled its members in the use of firearms and the United Englishmen corresponded with French revolutionaries and Irish rebels. There were also numerous attempts to overthrow George III. In 1794 the so-called Pop-gun Plot surfaced. It was alleged that there was a plan to assassinate the king at the theatre, using a poisoned dart fired from a pop-gun. Leading members of the radical London Corresponding Society, which urged parliamentary reform, were tried for treason, but were acquitted. However the situation on the streets was so turbulent that *habeas corpus* was suspended on several occasions. Then on 7 July 1798 James O'Coigley was hanged, drawn and quartered in Maidstone for 'compassing and imagining the death of the King and adhering to the King's enemies'. He had conspired to foment a rising in Britain and Ireland that was to coincide with an invasion by the French.

In 1802, Colonel Edward Despard, a disaffected Anglo-Irish army officer, planned to overthrow the British government by force of arms. He was known to both O'Coigley and Wolfe Tone, the Irish rebel who had cheated the gallows by cutting his own throat after the failed Irish insurrection of 1798. Despard's plan was to organize a mutiny of the Grenadier Guards, then capture the Tower of London and the Bank of England. This revolution was to be sparked off by the assassination of George III, using a huge Turkish cannon that sat at the back of the Admiralty. On 23 November 1802 chief clerk of police John Stafford led a large force of Bow Street Runners to the Oakley Arms in Lambeth. Surrounding the building they arrested Despard and his co-conspirators. Lord Nelson, who had fought alongside Despard in Honduras 24 years earlier, spoke in his defence and the jury recommended mercy 'on account of his former services'. Even so, the conspirators were sentenced to be hanged, drawn and quartered. In fact, they were publicly hanged, then beheaded, at Surrey County Gaol on 21 February 1803.

One of Despard's followers was Arthur Thistlewood. He was a member of the obscure Spencean Philanthropists, a libertarian society named after the radical Thomas Spence, who had been arrested for selling Tom Paine's *Rights of Man* in 1792. Many people in England sympathized with the American colonists, so revolution was in the air. The balance almost tipped after the Napoleonic Wars when the economy collapsed, wages fell and unemployment soared. Those Britons who had rallied to the revolutionary cause in France had now returned to England, bringing their revolutionary fervour with them.

In 1816 the Spenceans organized a public meeting at Spa Fields in Clerkenwell, where they intended to inflame the mob then march on the Bank of England. This plan failed, but a second rally was called two weeks later. Led by Spenceans wearing French Jacobin tricolour cockades, the mob marched on the City but they were intercepted by the police at the Royal Exchange. Any further resistance ended with the sound of cavalry hooves – the Life Guards, whose nickname was 'the Piccadilly butchers', had mounted a charge. They had brutally suppressed a riot in Piccadilly in 1810, hence the name.

A third rally at Spa Fields was organized. This time the mob would be armed. The self-styled Provisional Government aimed to send a ship to St Helena to bring Bonaparte back to London. Alerted by informants, the police swooped, arresting Thistlewood and his co-conspirators.

In Derbyshire, a stocking maker named Jeremiah Brandreth mustered 50 men and marched on Nottingham in the mistaken belief that it was already in the hands of revolutionaries. Confronted by a detachment of cavalry on the following day, the group fled. Brandreth was arrested six weeks later. Along with two of his co-conspirators, he was hanged and beheaded. Meanwhile, Thistlewood had been acquitted, although his plans for another Spa Field rebellion were thwarted when he was jailed for challenging the home secretary, Viscount Sidmouth, to a duel.

Thistlewood's release coincided with the 1819 'Peterloo Massacre', when a radical meeting at St Peter's Field in Manchester was cut down by the cavalry. This convinced Thistlewood that England was ripe for revolution. He planned another uprising at Spa Fields but it was organized as ineptly as before. At that point George III died, which caused a governmental crisis. Thistlewood planned to take advantage of this situation by murdering the cabinet when they met for dinner in Grosvenor Square on 23 February 1820. In the uprising that followed, George IV would be killed and Thistlewood would be named president. That

Sketch't by a Gentleman who was permitted to take a place upon the Building, the only lik
COL. EDWARD MARCUS DESPA
At the place of Execution upon the New Surrey Goal jus
ppeared when addressing the Spectators, a few minutes b ef
Platform dropped.
Pub by Alex Hogg 16 Paternoster row Feb 1803

ABOVE *Colonel Edward Marcus Despard was hanged for trying to start a revolution in England.*

night, as the conspirators assembled in a stable they had rented in Cato Street, off the Edgware Road, they were interrupted by the police. Thistlewood and his co-conspirators were found guilty of high treason. It was the last time that English offenders would be sentenced to be hanged, drawn and quartered. In the event, the rebels were 'only' hanged and decapitated.

LEFT *Jeremiah Brandreth led the Luddites in Nottingham. He was hanged in 1817, then beheaded.*

THE ROYAL MARRIAGES ACT

The Royal Marriages Act of 1772 makes it illegal for any member of the British royal family – defined as all of the descendants of George II – under the age of 25 to marry without the consent of the ruling monarch. Any member of the royal family over the age of 25 who has been refused the sovereign's consent can marry one year after they have given notice of their intention to the Privy Council, unless Parliament passes an act against the marriage in the meantime. As prince of Wales George IV did not ask his father's permission to marry Maria Fitzherbert, the marriage was invalid. Even if the marriage had been legal, the fact that Mrs Fitzherbert was a Catholic would have prevented George IV from succeeding. Such a situation was forbidden by the Act of Settlement.

In 1785, George secretly married a Roman Catholic, Maria Fitzherbert, which was illegal under the Royal Marriages Act of 1772. Parliament would only pay his debts if he married Princess Caroline of Brunswick. The wedding took place in 1795, but it was a disaster. In 1796, shortly after the birth of their only child, Princess Charlotte, the couple separated. Caroline was excluded from court during her husband's regency and in 1814 she moved to Italy, where she maintained an adulterous relationship with an Italian soldier named Bartolomeo Pergami.

When George came to the throne in 1820 he did all he could to persuade Caroline to stay on the Continent, but she returned to England. Parliament then introduced a bill that would strip her of her title and grant the king a divorce. Intimate details of her love life emerged during her trial before the House of Lords. But she was greeted by cheering crowds after admitting that she had indeed committed adultery with one man – the husband of Mrs Fitzherbert. The newspapers published word by word accounts of the trial and the caricaturists had a field day. Some of the prints were so obscene that the king spent over £2,500 in an attempt to suppress their publication. George IV was well known for his lecherous behaviour so Caroline was the focus of public sympathy. Although the Lords passed the bill by a narrow majority, it was then quietly dropped. However, Caroline was prevented from entering Westminster Abbey when her husband was crowned on 19 July 1821. She died mysteriously 19 days later.

George visited Hanover in 1821 and Scotland in 1822. He was the first British monarch to travel north of the border since 1650. Sir Walter Scott had been knighted two years earlier, about which the king later remarked, 'I shall always reflect with pleasure on Sir Walter Scott's having been the first creation of my reign.' George was also an admirer of Jane Austen, and it was he who donated his father's library to the British Museum. He then persuaded the Government to buy a collection of 38 paintings from the estate of the merchant John Julius Angerstein, which formed the nucleus of the National Gallery. Yet Brighton Pavilion perhaps comes first to mind when many people think of George IV. He first visited Brighton in 1783, searching for a seawater gout cure, and he went on to build the fanciful oriental-style creation that can be seen today.

George was little interested in government. He had courted Whig politicians in his youth, but that was mainly to annoy his father. When he became king he sided with the Tory second earl of Liverpool, prime minister from 1820 to 1827, who rejected

Catholic emancipation. However he liked the pro-emancipation George Canning, who became foreign secretary in 1822 and prime minister in 1827. But Canning died that year and it was up to Wellington to persuade the king to agree to the Catholic Relief Bill of 1829.

The king spent the last years of his life at Windsor Castle. He died on 26 June 1830. His only legitimate child, Princess Charlotte Augusta, had died in childbirth in 1817 so the crown passed to George's brother who became William IV. He was known as the 'Sailor King' or 'Silly Billy'.

LEFT *The novelist, poet and historian Sir Walter Scott revived Scottish national pride in the 19th century.*

The Sailor King

Born at Buckingham Palace on 21 August 1765, William IV (r.1830–7) was the third son of George III and Queen Charlotte and was not expected to succeed to the throne. At the age of 13 he began a career in the Royal Navy. He saw service in America and the West Indies, but ceased active service in 1780. Although he became admiral of the fleet in 1811 it was in an honorary capacity only. In 1789 he was created duke of Clarence and from the early 1790s until 1811 he lived with his mistress, the actress Dorothy Jordan. They had ten children who took the surname FitzClarence.

RIGHT *William IV – the 'Sailor King' – had ten children with his mistress, the actress Dorothy Jordan, but produced no legitimate heir.*

After the death of Princess Charlotte in 1817, the prince regent's only child, George's brothers scrambled to marry and produce heirs. That year, William married Princess Adelaide of Saxe-Meiningen. After George III's second son, the duke of York, died in 1827 William became heir. With the death of George IV he took the throne in June 1830. William was initially very popular because of his insistence on a simple coronation, which contrasted favourably with his brother's extravagance. He also worked amicably with the duke of Wellington's Tory government. But when the Tories lost the general election in August 1830 William came face to face with the reform crisis. The new Whig government, led by Earl Grey, was intent on pushing the Reform Bill through, in spite of strong opposition in the Commons and the Lords.

Another general election in 1831 gave the Whigs a majority in the Commons but the Lords continued to reject the Reform Bill. This threw the country into a political crisis and there were riots during the winter of 1831. William eventually agreed to create enough new peers to ensure that the Bill was passed in the House of Lords. The threat was enough to make the Lords back down.

The 1832 Reform Act abolished some of the worst abuses of the electoral system and extended the franchise to the middle classes. In the following year £20 million was set aside as compensation for the slave owners after the abolition of slavery in the British Empire. In 1834, the Poor Law was reformed for the first time since 1601, although the introduction of workhouses did little to help the needy. Then in 1835 local government was reformed.

William's more compliant attitude to reform was in total contrast to that of his brother George. It meant that he was the only European monarch of that time to survive the advent of democracy. The king had no legitimate children when he died on 20 June 1837 so he was succeeded by his niece Victoria (r.1837–1901).

BELOW *Earl Grey, leader of the Whig party, was the prime minister under William IV who passed the Reform Act, modernizing the franchise and electoral system.*

CHAPTER EIGHT

VIII

THE SAXE-COBURGS

THE SAXE-COBURGS

Victoria (1837–1901)

Edward VII (1901–10)

Dates show reign of monarch

LEFT *Queen Victoria's six children, 40 grandchildren and 37 great-grandchildren supplied most of the royal families of Europe.*

Empress of India

Queen Victoria (r.1837–1901) is the longest-reigning monarch in British history. Her grandfather, George III, had previously claimed the distinction. She was also the longest-living British monarch when she died. However, in 2007 that particular record was broken by Elizabeth II (see pages 198–205). During her reign, Victoria's immense empire doubled in size. She oversaw vast changes in society and gave her name to the Victorian age.

Victoria was born at Kensington Palace on 24 May 1819. She was the only child of Edward, duke of Kent, and Victoria Maria Louisa of Saxe-Coburg. Her father died when she was eight months old and his role was taken by her uncle, Leopold of Saxe-Coburg, the widower of Princess Charlotte Augusta. Leopold went on to become king of the Belgians (r.1831–65).

Queen Victoria succeeded her uncle William IV in 1837, at the age of 18, and her reign continued for the rest of the century. She could not ascend the shared throne of Hanover, however. According to Salic Law female heirs were not allowed, so her unpopular uncle Ernest, duke of Cumberland, became Ernest Augustus I.

The new queen inherited the Whig Lord Melbourne as prime minister. He became her political mentor and she became an ardent Whig. After he was

ABOVE *Queen Victoria was just 18 when she came to the throne. She reigned for 63 years at the height of Britain's imperial power.*

discredited in the Bedchamber Crisis, she turned for political advice to her first cousin, Prince Albert of Saxe-Coburg-Gotha, strengthening the Saxe-Coburg influence in her life. They married in February 1840 and for the next 20 years they lived in close harmony. Victoria gave birth to nine children, many of whom married into the monarchies of Europe.

Because he was a German, Prince Albert never really won the favour of the British public. He became a British subject but he was never made a peer. Only after 17 years of marriage was he given official recognition, when he received the title of Prince Consort. However, Victoria relied heavily on Albert's counsel and it was during his lifetime that she was most active as a ruler.

While Victoria was a hot-blooded young woman, Albert was cool and Germanic. He raised the royal family to the pinnacle of respectability and he also influenced British life in many other ways. For instance, he introduced the Christmas tree from his native Germany and he organized the Great Exhibition of 1851 in Hyde Park. Its centrepiece, the Crystal Palace, was later moved to Sydenham Hill in south London, where it remained until it burned down in 1936. The Great Exhibition attracted six million visitors and made a profit of £186,000. This money was used to buy 87 acres of land in South Kensington where the Victoria and Albert Museum, the Science Museum, Imperial College, the Royal College of Music and the Royal Albert Hall were built.

Victoria never fully recovered from Albert's death in 1861. For many years afterwards she remained secluded in her royal residences – Windsor, Balmoral and Osborne House on the Isle of Wight, which was built by Prince Albert. If she ventured abroad it was to the French

THE BEDCHAMBER CRISIS

During her childhood, Victoria was dominated by her widowed mother and her lover, the Irish upstart Sir John Conroy. The pair aimed to rule the country themselves when Victoria became queen. However, Victoria was made of sterner stuff. She found protection in her German governess, Louise Lehzen, and when she became Queen Victoria, gave orders to exclude Conroy from the court.

But Sir John was not a man easily thwarted and Victoria soon began to suspect that Lady Flora Hastings, one of her ladies of the bedchamber, was acting as his spy. After spending Christmas in Scotland in 1838, Lady Flora returned to London in a carriage shared with Conroy. Back at court, it was soon noticed that her abdomen was enlarged. She was also suffering from stomach pains. When she refused to be examined by the royal physician Sir James Clark 'with her stays off' it was concluded that she was pregnant.

When Lady Flora finally submitted to an examination, it was found that she was still technically a virgin, even though her womb was enlarged. But Victoria clung on to her belief in Flora's misconduct with Conroy and the rumour that she was pregnant still circulated. The source of the gossip proved to be the other ladies of the bedchamber.

All of this coincided with a government crisis. Melbourne's administration fell in 1839 and Victoria invited Sir Robert Peel to form a government. According to precedent Victoria was obliged to dismiss the ladies of the bedchamber after a change of government, but she refused to do so. Peel then resigned and Melbourne, Victoria's favourite, resumed. His administration lasted until 1841, to Victoria's satisfaction.

ABOVE *Lady Flora Hastings, centre of the 'bedchamber crisis' which made the new queen deeply unpopular.*

Victoria's treatment of Flora Hastings made her very unpopular. She was hissed at by the crowd at Ascot and the mobs called her 'Mrs Melbourne'. The general feeling was that the prime minister was more than just an adviser. Indeed, Melbourne had something of a reputation. He had survived two scandalous divorces and had once complimented the young queen on her 'full and fine bust'. She was mortified at his final downfall in 1841.

Eventually, Victoria bowed to public pressure. On 26 June 1839 she went to see Lady Hastings, who was by then on her deathbed. Victoria recorded in her diary:

> 'I found poor Lady Flora stretched on a couch looking as thin as anybody can be who is still alive, but the body very much swollen like a person who is with child.'

When Flora died on 5 July it was discovered that she had a tumour on her liver, which had remained undiagnosed by Sir James Clark. The *Morning Post* voiced the view of many when it accused the queen of 'the most revolting virulence and indecency'. The goodwill that had attended her coronation on 28 June 1838 seemed to have totally evaporated.

RIGHT *Queen Victoria goes riding at Windsor, accompanied by Lord Melbourne, her trusted adviser.*

PRINCE ALBERT

Francis Albert Augustus Charles Emmanuel of Saxe-Coburg-Gotha was born on 26 August 1819 at Schloss Rosenau, in Bavaria. He was the youngest son of the duke of Saxe-Coburg-Gotha. When he was seven years old, his father divorced his mother on the grounds of adultery. She was sent to live in Switzerland and was forbidden to see her children again. Albert was educated at Bonn University and in 1840 he married his cousin, Queen Victoria. The marriage was unpopular with the Government, to the extent that Parliament granted him a smaller allowance than his predecessors.

Following the death of Lord Melbourne in 1848 Albert became Victoria's principal adviser as well as her private secretary. He encouraged her to take a greater interest in social welfare by inviting Lord Shaftesbury, the factory reformer, to Buckingham Palace. Albert's constitutional position was a difficult one and he was never popular with the public. He was not formally recognized by the nation until 1857, when he became Prince Consort.

Albert took an active interest in science, the arts, trade and industry. Perhaps his greatest achievement was the masterminding of the Great Exhibition of 1851. Although the exhibition was designed to celebrate Britain's industrial leadership, and the expansion of its empire, the French won most of the prizes. But foreign success did little to dent British pride. The enormous profits from the venture went towards the founding of the South Kensington museum complex.

ABOVE *Prince Albert, Victoria's husband, was unpopular, but the queen found him an invaluable adviser. He helped stabilize the monarchy after the disastrous Hanoverian era.*

In the autumn of 1861, when the American Civil War was in progress, Albert became involved in a diplomatic row between Britain and the United States. The British mail packet *Trent* was sailing from Havana to London with two Confederate envoys on board. While the *Trent* was at sea she was stopped by the USS *San Jacinto,* a Union frigate, and the Confederate envoys were removed. The incident brought the two nations close to war until Prince Albert intervened. President Lincoln then disavowed the action and released the envoys, who continued their passage to London. All was in vain, because they failed to secure diplomatic recognition for the Confederacy.

When Albert died suddenly of typhoid on 14 December 1861, Victoria was overwhelmed by grief. She remained in widow's weeds for the rest of her life. A number of monuments were commissioned in Albert's honour, including the Royal Albert Memorial in Kensington Gardens. The main structure was completed in 1868. Albert and Victoria had nine children, most of whom married into the royal houses of Europe.

THE GREAT EXHIBITION

The French Industrial Exposition of 1844 had been highly successful and Britain wanted to respond. But the cost of a British version would have been prohibitive. Then Prince Albert came up with the idea of a self-financing exhibition that would open its doors to the world. The Great Exhibition of the Works of Industry of All Nations was the first-ever international exhibition of manufactured goods.

The exhibition was open from 1 May to 15 October 1851 and it was visited by six million people. It was housed in an innovative glass and cast-iron structure, the 'Crystal Palace', which had been designed by Joseph Paxton, head gardener and greenhouse designer. Paxton's design was essentially a giant greenhouse, which could be easily and quickly assembled from identical, interchangeable pieces. This lowered the materials cost considerably. The design was initially rejected but public pressure eventually forced its acceptance.

Rival architects claimed that the building would collapse from the resonance set up by the feet of large crowds. So a model was built on which workmen walked back and forth, first in time and then out of step. Then they all jumped up and down. As a final test, a troop of soldiers marched heavily through. The structure survived, although a dome had to be added to accommodate some very tall trees.

The finished building was 1,848 feet (563 m) long and 408 feet (124 m) wide, with an extra wing 936 feet (285 m) by 48 feet (15 m) sticking out on one side. A grand avenue and upstairs galleries ran along the whole length of the building. Altogether, the Crystal Palace covered an area of 18 acres (7 hectares) – not including the 5 acres (2 hectares) of upper galleries. That is six times the area of St Paul's. Huge quantities of materials were used in the construction of the building – 550 tons of wrought iron, 3,500 tons of cast iron, 900,000 feet (274,000 m) of glass and 600,000 feet (183,000 m) of wooden planking.

The Crystal Palace was completed on time and on budget. So many tickets were sold in advance that the exhibition made a profit before it even opened. Admission costs ranged from three guineas (£3.15) to one shilling (5p), according to the date of the visit. The shilling tickets were a particular success – four and a half million were sold.

There were 100,000 exhibits from 14,000 exhibitors, some from as far away as China. A dazzling range of goods was displayed. Silks, clocks, furniture, farm machinery – the list went on and on. As the leading industrial nation of the day Britain contributed over half of the exhibits, although the French scooped many of the awards. The 560 exhibits from the United States included the Colt repeating pistol, false teeth, artificial legs, Goodyear's rubber and chewing tobacco. Popular British exhibits included powerful new steam engines, hydraulic presses, pumps and automated cotton spinning machines.

ABOVE *The Crystal Palace was built in Hyde Park to house the Great Exhibition.*

CHARTISM

Although Victoria became a popular monarch towards the end of her life, her reign was marked by the growth of republicanism. This wave of popular feeling found early expression in the Chartist Movement, which took its name from the 'People's Charter' of 1838. The document was drafted by William Lovett during the economic depression of 1837–8 and it quickly became a rallying point for social reform agitators. Chartism had six main aims:

- Voting by secret ballot.
- Annual Parliamentary elections.
- The abolition of a property requirement for MPs.
- Salaries for MPs.
- Universal male suffrage.
- Electoral districts of equal size.

A national convention of 53 delegates met in London on 4 February 1839. Although the law prohibited gatherings of more than 50 people, the organizers made sure that not all of them

ABOVE *Chartist leader William Lovett, largely responsible for drafting the 'People's Charter'.*

ABOVE *Queen Victoria and her Indian servant Abdul Karim listening to a dispatch from the front line during the Boer War.*

were present at the same time. Some delegates favoured using violence to promote reform – others called for a general strike. There was even talk of electing a separate 'people's parliament'. The convention adopted a provocative slogan – 'peaceably if we may, forcibly if we must'. The movement was joined by a number of radical Irishmen, particularly those pushing for Catholic emancipation.

There was general unrest throughout the spring of 1839 and troops were called in to maintain order, particularly in the north. Rioting was particularly prevalent in Birmingham where Lovett, among others, was arrested. The Chartists gathered over 1.25 million signatures in support of their aims. These signatures, together with the Charter, were presented to Parliament when it gathered in July 1839. Although the Charter was supported by Benjamin Disraeli, the House of Commons rejected it by a vote of 235 to 46.

Following the failure of national action, the movement became more localized. There was an armed uprising in Newport in which 24 protesters were killed. Its leaders were transported to Australia. Then in 1842 the Chartists gathered another three million signatures together. Again Parliament rejected their demands. In 1848, there was another national convention and a further petition was presented. After this final failure the Chartist Movement died out.

The revival of the economy had robbed the reform movement of its main driving force. Radical Chartists found a new home in the nascent socialist movement. Karl Marx published *The Communist Manifesto* in 1848 and moved to London in the following year. But the Chartist Movement cannot be judged as a failure because five of the Chartists' six demands have been secured. We have yet to see annual parliaments.

CHARTIST DEMONSTRATION!!

"PEACE and ORDER" is our MOTTO!

TO THE WORKING MEN OF LONDON.

Fellow Men,—The Press having misrepresented and vilified us and our intentions, the Demonstration Committee therefore consider it to be their duty to state that the grievances of us (the Working Classes) are deep and our demands just. We and our families are pining in misery, want, and starvation! We demand a fair day's wages for a fair day's work! We are the slaves of capital—we demand protection to our labour. We are political serfs—we demand to be free. We therefore invite all well disposed to join in our peaceful procession on

MONDAY NEXT, April 10,

As it is for the good of all that we seek to remove the evils under which we groan.

The following are the places of Meeting of THE CHARTISTS, THE TRADES, THE IRISH CONFEDERATE & REPEAL BODIES:

East Division on Stepney Green at 8 o'clock; City and Finsbury Division on Clerkenwell Green at 9 o'clock; West Division in Russell Square at 9 o'clock; and the South Division in Peckham Fields at 9 o'clock, and proceed from thence to Kennington Common.

Signed on behalf of the Committee, JOHN ARNOTT, *Sec.*

ABOVE *The handbill calling supporters to the Chartist demonstration on Kennington Common.*

RIGHT *The Chartists were outspoken. But Parliament ignored them, though their demands have now largely been granted.*

Riviera. However, she found solace in the company of her Scottish gillie, John Brown. After his death in 1883, her Indian servant Abdul Karim was a close companion. The queen remained in mourning until the Golden Jubilee of 1887, even though her withdrawal from public life made her unpopular. During the late 1870s and 1880s she gradually returned to public view and was restored to favour with the British public. Nevertheless, she avoided public ceremonials where possible because she was the target of six assassination attempts during her lifetime.

When Disraeli became prime minister in 1864, the British Empire was growing apace. It included Canada, Australia, India, Burma, New Zealand, much of the Caribbean and large parts of Africa. Then in 1875 Disraeli bought a controlling interest in the Suez Canal, effectively annexing Egypt. After the Indian Mutiny of 1857 the government of India had been transferred from the East India Company to the Crown, so Disraeli was able to bestow the rank of empress of India on his queen. It was added to her list of titles on 1 May 1876.

During Victoria's reign, Britain remained largely uninvolved in European affairs, with the one great exception of the Crimean War (1853–6). Britain, France, the Ottoman Empire

BELOW *Queen Victoria presents a medal to Sir Thomas Troubridge who lost his leg at the Battle of Inkerman during the Crimean War.*

THE RISE OF THE BRITISH EMPIRE

By 1922 Britain exercised control over 458 million people, who were spread over a quarter of the earth's surface. The task of creating this huge empire had been greatly eased by the fact that Britain had often been politically stable, so government agencies were able to concentrate their efforts abroad. And the occasional political upheaval aided colonization, because floods of dissidents then left the country to seek their fortune in the growing empire.

The first overseas settlements were established in the 16th century. Then rivalry with the French in the 17th century resulted in an explosion of colonies in North America and the Caribbean. Jamaica was taken from Spain by Cromwell's forces in 1655 and the Hudson's Bay Company spread into northwestern Canada in the 1670s.

Meanwhile the East India Company received its first Royal Charter in 1600. It began establishing trading posts in India, then extended further eastwards to include the Straits Settlements at Penang, Singapore, Malacca and Labuan in Malaya. Although they were acquired by private individuals or companies, these trading centres gradually fell under government administration.

The first permanent British settlement on the African continent was established at James Island in

ABOVE *A British grandee rides in an Indian procession – Britain had a presence in the subcontinent for over three centuries.*

the Gambia River in 1661. Sierra Leone then became a British colony in 1792. The Cape of Good Hope also became a colony in 1806, which allowed the Dutch-speaking Boers to open up the interior under British control. The Treaty of Paris of 1763 enabled the British to retain the possessions they had taken from the French in Canada, the Caribbean and India in the Seven Years' War. Robert Clive became governor of Bengal in 1765 and over the following century Britain took over the rest of the Indian subcontinent.

With all of this going on the loss of the thirteen American colonies in the 18th century was not such a huge blow. In any case, North America was seen as a vast barren wilderness. Britain was far more interested in the fertile West Indies, where sugar cane could be grown. And the British hold on Canada was bolstered by loyalists leaving the newly independent United States.

The new settlements in Australia that began in 1788 were a further compensation for the loss of the American colonies. The criminals that might have been transported to North America were now sent to Australia. The Napoleonic wars brought a host of possessions into the empire – Trinidad and Ceylon (now Sri Lanka) in 1802 and Malta, St Lucia, Tobago and Mauritius in 1814. They were joined by New Zealand in 1840, followed by Fiji, Tonga, Papua, Cyprus, Sudan, Nigeria, the Gold Coast (now Ghana), the Gambia, Malawi, Northern Rhodesia (now Zambia) and Southern Rhodesia (now Zimbabwe). Other former German colonies were annexed after World War I.

While countries were taken over piecemeal, often through commercial ventures, integration was achieved by the Colonial Office. Larger colonies – Canada, Australia, New Zealand and South Africa – were given self-governing dominion status. The empire was dissolved after the Second World War. Most of its former members joined the Commonwealth, a loose association of nations.

Throughout Victoria's reign, Britain was evolving into a constitutional monarchy. The queen had few powers and she was expected to remain above party politics – but she often expressed her views very forcefully in private. Despite her seclusion she oversaw the Mines Act of 1842, which prevented women and children from being employed underground; various Factory Acts that again reduced the exploitation of women and children; the Education Act of 1870 that laid the foundations of elementary education; the Public Health and Artisans' Dwelling Acts of 1875; the Trade Union Acts of 1871 and 1876; and the Reform Acts of 1867 and 1884.

Ten prime ministers served under her – Lord Melbourne, Sir Robert Peel, Lord John Russell, Lord

and the Kingdom of Sardinia (which joined Italy in 1861) were united against Russia in this conflict. The Victoria Cross, the highest award for valour, was introduced at the end of the war. To this day the medal is made from Russian guns captured at Sebastopol.

Victoria's Golden and Diamond Jubilees, in 1887 and 1897, were celebrated with great enthusiasm, although the queen refused to wear the crown or robes of state. Instead, she preferred to appear in a simple landau, wearing a bonnet laced with diamonds. It pleased her to play the role of the 'widow of Windsor'.

Derby, Lord Aberdeen, Viscount Palmerston, Benjamin Disraeli, William Ewart Gladstone, Lord Rosebery and Lord Salisbury. Melbourne and Disraeli were the most influential. She hated Gladstone who, she said, addressed her as if she were a public meeting.

Victoria died at Osborne House on 22 January 1901. By then she was related, either directly or by marriage, to the royal houses of Germany, Russia, Greece, Romania, Sweden, Denmark, Norway and Belgium. Kaiser Wilhelm II – 'Willy' – was her grandson, while Tsar Nicholas II – 'dear Nicky' – was the husband of her granddaughter Alexandra.

LEFT *Edward VII is better known to history as Bertie, Queen Victoria's champagne-swilling, gambling and womanizing son, and the prince of Wales.*

'Bertie' Ascends the Throne

Queen Victoria was succeeded by her son Edward VII (r.1901–10), who was known throughout his wayward youth as 'Bertie'. He was 59 years old when he came to the throne. Although his father had died nearly 40 years earlier, Victoria had kept Bertie well away from affairs of state. He might have been a Saxe-Coburg by birth, but she was afraid that his Hanoverian blood would show itself. He lived up to her every expectation.

Denied a role, he devoted most of his energies to chasing women and getting involved in scandals.

Edward was born at Buckingham Palace on 9 November 1841. He was the first heir presumptive to be born to a reigning monarch since George IV in 1762. From his birth, his parents prepared him to rule so he was subjected to a strict regime. He attended both Oxford and Cambridge and he served briefly in the army. After a drunken mess party at

the Curragh military camp near Dublin in March 1861, a naked actress named Nellie Clifden turned up in his bed. When the story got out, Albert travelled up to Cambridge to chastise his son, who had returned there as a student.

Albert died of typhoid only two weeks later. For the rest of her life, Victoria blamed Bertie for the early death of her beloved Albert.

After Albert's death the grieving Victoria almost completely withdrew from public life so Edward represented her at state occasions. But he was still given no opportunity to participate in government matters. He was over 50 years old before Victoria told him anything of cabinet proceedings, although he was able to sit in the House of Lords. Having developed little interest in politics, he became a leader of London society. His time was spent eating, drinking, gambling, shooting, racing, sailing and entertaining at Marlborough House, his private residence in Pall Mall. He also spent a good deal of time womanizing on the Continent and frequented brothels on both sides of the Channel.

In 1863 Edward married Princess Alexandra of Denmark and they had six children, five of whom survived to adulthood. Alexandra put up with a series of long-term, high-profile mistresses, who included the actress Lily Langtry and Alice Keppel. In 1870, Edward was subpoenaed to appear at the divorce trial of Sir Charles Mordaunt. However, the case foundered when the strain of the proceedings drove the already unstable Lady Mordaunt insane. Although Edward was not directly named as co-respondent, the crowds booed him when he arrived at the Olympic Theatre with Alexandra. They did the same at Ascot, after which a meeting in Hyde Park called for the abolition of the monarchy. Gladstone suggested that Edward should be made viceroy of Ireland. He would then be out of the country. But Queen Victoria disagreed. In October 1871 Edward almost died of typhoid. When he recovered, Gladstone took the opportunity to organize a series of celebrations. Edward's popularity was restored and he then made a royal tour of India.

Back in England in 1891, he was subpoenaed again. This time it was the Tranby Croft affair. When Edward had been visiting Tranby Croft, a country

LEFT *Edward enjoys a private show at Chatsworth in 1901. He is sitting between the Duchess of Devonshire and his mistress Mrs Alice Keppel.*

house near Doncaster, he had been present at a game of baccarat, then illegal in Britain. During the game, Sir William Gordon-Cumming was accused of cheating, so he took the matter to court in an attempt to restore his good name. He lost but so did Edward, because further salacious details of his disreputable private life were revealed by the case.

Edward's eldest son Albert Victor, or 'Eddy', attracted even more scandal than his father. Reputed to have had

Mistress Keppel

ABOVE *Mrs Alice Keppel, the last mistress of Edward VII, was the great-grandmother of Camilla, duchess of Cornwall, the second wife of Charles, prince of Wales.*

homosexual affairs at Cambridge, he was also a member of the notorious Hundred Guineas Club in Cleveland Street. The club was the subject of the infamous Cleveland Street Scandal in 1889, in which it was identified as a male brothel. Eddy's name was kept out of the proceedings, but one of those named was Lord Euston, who was aide-de-camp at Edward VII's coronation in 1901. Some even thought Eddy was Jack the Ripper. Eddy died from influenza during the pandemic of 1892.

Despite all of the scandals that had surrounded Bertie as prince of Wales, his popularity was restored by his coronation. It had been arranged for 26 June, but he became ill before the event, almost dying from appendicitis. The ceremony had to be postponed but vast quantities of exquisite food had already been prepared.

It was a red-letter day for the poor of London's East End – they were on the receiving end of 2,500 quails, 300 legs of mutton, oysters, prawns, snipe, *consommé de faisan aux quenelles* and sole poached in Chablis. By the time Edward was eventually crowned on 9 August, he had risen greatly in the public's esteem.

Edward VII threw himself into his new role with gusto, restoring a sparkle to the monarchy that had been lost with his father's death 40 years earlier. Although Edward was seen as the first truly constitutional monarch, he handled his ministers with great dexterity. However, his forte was foreign affairs. As prince of Wales he had travelled widely in France, Italy, Spain, Germany, Denmark, Sweden, Belgium, Russia, India, Canada and the United States. Related to most of Europe's royalty, he was known as the 'Uncle of Europe' – so foreign policy negotiations were a family affair. A well-received address during a state visit to Paris helped pave the way for the Anglo-French *Entente Cordiale* of 1904. The Boer War was brought to an end early in his reign, he was the first British monarch to visit Russia and in 1902 he founded the Order of Merit – a reward for those who had distinguished themselves in science, art or literature.

A constitutional crisis occupied Edward in the final year of his life, when the Liberals were in power. In his 1909 budget the chancellor of the exchequer, David Lloyd George, was trying to tax the rich in order to pay for old-age

THE *ENTENTE CORDIALE*

The *Entente Cordiale* was signed in London on 8 April 1904 by Lord Lansdowne and Paul Cambon. Although it was the idea of Théophile Delcassé, the French foreign minister, the informal treaty took shape during a visit to France by Edward VII in 1903. A number of long-standing issues between Britain and France were resolved by the *Entente Cordiale*. The two countries were also able to present a united front to belligerent Germany in the years before the First World War.

Colonial issues were also at the forefront of the agreement. The *Entente* granted Great Britain freedom of action in Egypt, although French archaeologists and scholars maintained certain rights. In exchange, Britain agreed not to interfere with the French position in Morocco. Britain also ceded the Los Islands off French Guinea, redrew the Nigerian border in France's favour and conceded French control of the upper Gambia valley. France renounced its exclusive rights to fisheries off Newfoundland and then settled a rivalry between British and French colonialists in the New Hebrides, a group of islands in the South Pacific. Britain and France also came to an agreement over their colonial possessions in southeast Asia – France took possession of Indochina while Britain received Siam (Thailand) and Burma.

France had already signed an alliance with Russia in 1892. When Britain did the same in 1907 a Triple *Entente* was automatically established. The three nations could now co-operate with each other against Germany, the common enemy.

ABOVE *In the* Entente Cordiale *Britain turned her back on her traditional ally Germany and allied herself with France, a traditional enemy.*

pensions for the poor. It was called the 'People's Budget'. The proposal was vetoed by the House of Lords but the Liberals countered by threatening to reduce the power of the upper house. That did the trick – the motion was passed. But the Liberals still reduced the power of the Lords by means of the Parliament Act of 1911.

Edward died on 6 May 1910, after a series of heart attacks. When it became clear that he was dying Queen Alexandra gave orders that Edward's mistress, Mrs Keppel, should be sent for immediately. Alice Keppel was the great-grandmother of Camilla Parker-Bowles, the wife of the current prince of Wales and duchess of Cornwall.

CHAPTER NINE

THE WINDSORS

THE HOUSE OF WINDSOR

George V (1910–36)

Edward VIII (1936–abdicated December 1936)

George VI (1936–52)

Elizabeth II (1952–)

Dates show reign of monarch

LEFT *George VI and his daughter Princess Elizabeth, later Queen Elizabeth II, have preserved the monarchy into the modern age.*

A Change of Name

Edward VII was succeeded by his second son George V (r.1910–36), who was born at Marlborough House on 3 June 1865. At the age of 18 George joined the Royal Navy and served around the world. But the death of his elder brother in 1892 meant that his life could no longer be risked on active service. He had to return home, where he was groomed for his future role. In the following year, he married his elder brother's fiancée, Princess Mary of Teck. They went on to have six children.

George's reign began in the middle of a constitutional crisis. At that time the predominantly Conservative House of Lords had the power to veto any legislation that was put forward by the Commons. The Liberal government, who won a second election in 1910, were attempting to curb this excessive power by introducing the Parliament Bill. When the Lords again voted against the Bill, the king promised to aid the government by creating a large number of Liberal peers. At that point the Lords backed down and the Parliament Act was passed in 1911. No new peers were needed.

In the same year George visited India, the only king-emperor to do so.

Unlike his flamboyant predecessors, George preferred to spend his time at Sandringham, where he lived the quiet life of a Norfolk squire. He did not even live in the main house, but chose to stay in the modest York Cottage that had been built by his father. An avid stamp collector, his collection contained an example of every British Empire stamp that had ever been issued. However, he could be lured out of rural isolation when duty called. In 1914 he attempted to solve the problem of Irish Home rule by hosting a conference at Buckingham Palace. But the opposition of the Ulster Unionists meant that a solution could not be reached. The 1916 Easter Rising in Dublin then led to civil war and partition. Ireland became two countries in 1922 – the Irish Free State in the south, which became a dominion, and

BELOW *Nicholas II of Russia and George V of Britain were first cousins, but George felt offering the deposed Romanovs asylum in Britain would endanger his own throne.*

to turn a blind eye to the plight of another first cousin, Kaiser Wilhelm II of Germany, who was assailed by calls for his execution. Fortunately Wilhelm found asylum in the Netherlands, where he died in 1941.

George found the downfall of his cousins all the most distressing because he was very much a family man. He was always extremely close to his unmarried sister, Princess Victoria of Wales. They spoke on the telephone every day. When she died on 3 December 1935 the king was very deeply affected. Her death overshadowed the Christmas celebrations at Sandringham that year.

George saw a great many changes in his lifetime. For example, he invited Ramsay MacDonald to form the first Labour government in 1924. Then following the world slump in 1929 he put forward the idea of a national government. The coalition formed by the Labour, Conservative and Liberal parties won the 1931 election. Also in 1931, the Statute of Westminster allowed parliaments in the dominions to pass laws without reference to the United Kingdom. This paradoxically increased the importance of the monarchy, since the only thing linking the dominions to Britain was their common allegiance to the crown.

George was also the first monarch to make a radio broadcast – he made a Christmas speech in 1932 that became an annual event. A few years

Ulster, which remained part of the United Kingdom.

Public respect for George V greatly increased during the First World War. He made many journeys to the front and tirelessly visited hospitals, factories and dockyards. During one visit to France he was thrown from his horse, fracturing his pelvis. But by 1917 anti-German feeling was running high. His Battenberg cousins had already changed their family name to Mountbatten – George followed their example by ordering the name of the royal family to be changed from Saxe-Coburg-Gotha to Windsor. This was a shrewd move because the First World War had put an end to many European monarchies.

A name change was not enough in those times. When George's first cousin, Tsar Nicholas II, was deposed during the Russian Revolution of 1917 the king felt unable to offer the Romanovs asylum in Britain. As a result, the Bolsheviks massacred the Russian royal family at Yekaterinburg in 1918. George also had

later, in 1935, India gained a measure of self-governance. George celebrated his Silver Jubilee in the same year and was much affected by the warmth displayed towards him by the ordinary people. 'I had no idea I was so popular,' he said to Robert Menzies, the Australian prime minister.

The king had never been a well man. In the navy he had suffered badly from seasickness and in 1928 he was found to be suffering from a severe respiratory illness. As his condition deteriorated, his eldest son the prince of Wales was called back from a visit to South Africa. He had to be ready to succeed at short notice. An operation was performed to drain the fluid from George's lungs and his life hung in the balance for a few days. However, he made a gradual recovery in a convalescent home at Bognor, on the south coast. Although Bognor acquired its 'Regis' suffix because of his stay, the charms of the seaside town had little appeal for the king. George,

who was a gruff and difficult patient, returned to Windsor Castle as soon as he felt able. He suffered two relapses but stubbornly refused to return to Bognor for further convalescence. When pushed on the point, he famously exclaimed, 'Bugger Bognor!'

George V died at Sandringham on 20 January 1936. The cause of death was given as a bronchial illness. Fifty years later it was revealed that the royal physician, Lord Dawson of Penn, had administered a lethal dose of morphine and cocaine to the dying king in order that his death could be announced in the morning edition of *The Times,* rather than be first reported in 'less appropriate' evening newspapers.

After lying in state at Westminster Hall for four days, during which his four sons took turns guarding the bier, the king's body was buried in the Chapel of the Knights of the Garter at Windsor Castle. He was succeeded by his eldest son, Edward VIII.

BELOW *George V oversaw the formation of the National Government under Ramsay MacDonald following the economic chaos caused by the Great Depression.*

The Shortest Reign Since Edward V

Edward VIII was born on 23 June 1894 at White Lodge, Richmond, Surrey, the home of his maternal grandparents. He was christened Edward Albert Christian George Andrew Patrick David and was known in the family as David. The name Edward came from his paternal uncle, Albert Victor, duke of Clarence, who was known to the family as Eddy. Albert Victor had been engaged to Edward's mother before he died in 1892. Queen Victoria was still alive when Edward was born. She wrote proudly to her eldest daughter, Vicky, in Germany, that it was the first time in English history 'that there should be three direct heirs, as well as the sovereign alive'. Edward was educated by a private tutor at the family home of York Cottage on the Sandringham estate. Later he went to Dartmouth Naval College, where his younger brother, Bertie, joined him. When his father George V succeeded to the throne, Edward was given the traditional title of prince of Wales and was formally invested at Caernarfon Castle in July 1911, although he only reluctantly wore the 'preposterous rig' – a 'purple and miniver cloak and gold circlet' – that his mother had run up for him.

Edward joined the Grenadier Guards at the outbreak of the First World War. He expressed a wish to serve in the front lines, which was firmly opposed by his father, but he still managed to become a staff officer. He annoyed his father yet further by refusing to wear the medals that had been given to him by his uncle, Tsar Nicholas, on the grounds that he had not earned them.

The prince of Wales represented his father on a number of foreign tours throughout the 1920s, particularly within the empire. With his blond hair, Teutonic good looks and boyish charm, he had all the appeal of a film star. Visits to areas of high unemployment and deprivation in Britain during the economic depression of the early 1930s also made him very popular. As unemployment soared, he steered more than 200,000 men and women into occupational schemes.

ABOVE *The future King Edward VIII, known to his family as David, at the age of seven in 1901. Like his young brother Albert, the future George VI, he was trained as a sailor.*

ABOVE *Edward VIII, when prince of Wales, meeting Indian soldiers who had lost limbs fighting for Britain in World War I.*

While he was popular with the people, his relationship with his father remained strained. George V disliked his son's informal behaviour and the circles he moved in. The king was a stickler for morality but Edward had affairs with a number of married women during the 1920s. In an attempt to keep his son out of the public eye, George V gave him Fort Belvedere, near Sunningdale, an 18th-century house that belonged to the crown. The property obviously exerted an influence on Edward because he indulged his passion for horticulture in the gardens and woodlands there. However, he also used the house to entertain his friends from the 'fast set'. Through them he met American divorcee Wallis Warfield Simpson. Hearing of their affair, the king is reported to have told his prime minister Stanley Baldwin, 'After I am dead that boy will ruin himself in 12 months.'

Edward became king after the death of his father in January 1936. He opened Parliament in November and then toured some of the areas of high unemployment in South Wales. 'Something must be done to find these people work,' he said. This endeared him to the people, but his remark was not well received by the Government, who felt that the monarch should not be meddling in politics. It would not be a problem for long because they quickly found a way of getting rid of the king.

In November, Edward VIII informed prime minister Stanley Baldwin that he intended to marry Mrs Simpson as soon as her latest divorce was completed.

WALLIS SIMPSON

Born Bessie Wallis Warfield in Pennsylvania on 19 June 1896, she was the daughter of a successful businessman. Her first husband was Earl Winfield Spencer, a US Navy pilot who was also an alcoholic. The couple met and married in 1916 but separated in 1921. Wallis later joined her husband in China, where she spent some time before returning alone to the United States. Spencer and Wallis were divorced in 1927.

Wallis then met Ernest Simpson, a British businessman who had been born in the United States. After Simpson had divorced his wife the couple married in London in 1928. They became friendly with Lady Thelma Furness, a mistress of Edward, prince of Wales. On 10 January 1931 Furness invited them to her country house at Melton Mowbray, where they met the prince. Wallis and Edward began an affair in 1934.

After the prince became Edward VIII on 20 January 1936, Wallis Simpson sued for divorce from her second husband, apparently with the intention of marrying the king. The king's relationship with Wallis Simpson was already widely reported in the foreign press, although the British newspapers kept quiet about it. The prime minister, Stanley Baldwin, urged the king to consider the constitutional consequences of marrying a divorced woman. Cosmo Lang, the archbishop of Canterbury, also made it clear that he was strongly opposed to the king's

The Sketch

No. 2200.—Vol. CLXIX.   WEDNESDAY, MARCH 27, 1935.   ONE SHILLING.

MRS. ERNEST SIMPSON.

ABOVE *The front cover of* The Sketch *in March 1935, featuring a portrait by Dorothy Wilding of Mrs Ernest Wallis Simpson.*

relationship. Although Edward was warmly supported by Winston Churchill and Lord Beaverbrook, he knew that marrying Wallis Simpson would be unpopular with the British public.

The Government was also aware that Wallis Simpson was involved in other sexual relationships. Among her lovers, she counted a married car mechanic and salesman called Guy Trundle and Edward Fitzgerald, duke of Leinster. More crucially, the Federal Bureau of Investigation believed that Wallis Simpson was sleeping with Joachim von Ribbentrop, the German Ambassador to the court of St James, and that she was passing secret information obtained from the king to the Nazis.

Although Wallis apparently urged him not to abdicate, on 10 December 1936 Edward VIII renounced the throne 'for myself and my descendants'. On the following day he made a radio broadcast in which he told the nation that he had abdicated because he found he could not 'discharge the duties of king as I would wish to do without the help and support of the woman I love'.

Edward then went to Austria where he stayed with friends until Wallis Simpson obtained her divorce. On 3 June 1937 the couple were married at the Château de Candé in France. They stayed together until Edward died in Paris in 1972.

THE ABDICATION CRISIS

In the summer of 1936, Edward VIII took a holiday with Mrs Simpson on board his chartered yacht *Nahlin* in the Mediterranean. The British press remained silent, although the romantic interlude was widely covered in foreign newspapers. Rumours circulated that the couple would marry as soon as Mrs Simpson's second divorce came through. On 15 October the king's secretary Sir Alexander Hardinge learned that Mrs Simpson's petition for divorce was about to be heard in Ipswich – he immediately informed the prime minister Stanley Baldwin. Baldwin told the king that the British press were bound to lift their self-imposed censorship after this development. He suggested that the king should persuade Mrs Simpson to drop her divorce and go abroad for six months. The king replied that the divorce was a private matter for Mrs Simpson.

On 27 October Mrs Simpson obtained a *decree nisi,* but the British press still remained silent. Hardinge then warned the duke of York, who was next in line to the throne, that there was a possibility that his brother might abdicate. As the crisis came to a head, Hardinge warned the king that if he married Mrs Simpson the Government might resign over the matter. Baldwin believed British public opinion would be against the marriage. The dominions were canvassed for their opinion but the reaction was also hostile. This was an important moment because Edward VIII was the first monarch to be head of state of each dominion individually. For once the king was concerned: he had been popular in the dominions because of his modern ways. There were other reasons why Edward should not marry Mrs Simpson. He was the head of the Church of England, which did not allow divorcees to remarry in church, and there was no recent precedent for the monarch to marry a commoner.

Lord Rothermere, owner of the *Daily Mail*, suggested that Edward and Mrs Simpson had a morganatic marriage, in which Mrs Simpson would marry the king but not become queen. But while the Royal Marriages Act allowed the king to marry someone who would be queen, a morganatic marriage would require an Act of Parliament. This would have sparked off an extensive debate in Parliament, which was known to be hostile to the king's marriage. Nevertheless the king formally put the proposal of a morganatic marriage to Baldwin on 25 November. The dominions and the opposition were also formally consulted. All parties agreed that Mrs Simpson would make an unsuitable queen and that a morganatic marriage was not an acceptable compromise.

On 1 December the bishop of Bradford, Alfred Blunt, told his diocesan conference that the king was in need of divine grace. Although the bishop later said that he had never even heard of Mrs Simpson, his remarks were interpreted as a reference to the affair. The British press broke its self-imposed silence and printed calls for the king's abdication. Mrs Simpson was against an abdication, preferring the morganatic solution. If that was not possible, she said, she did not find her position of *maîtresse en titre* unappealing. The day after the story broke in the press, she left for Cannes.

ABOVE *The front page of the* Daily Mirror *of 11 December 1936 showing the new king, George VI, arriving at his home at 145 Piccadilly.*

'I am sure there is only one solution,' she said. 'That is for me to remove myself from the king's life. That is what I am doing now.' However, she later phoned the king, urging him to fight for his rights and ignore what the Government said about his marriage.

Edward hoped to appeal directly to the British people by making a radio broadcast. Baldwin and the cabinet opposed this move. While not explicitly advising the king to give up Wallis Simpson, they insisted that they were the representatives of the public in this matter. The king, isolated at Fort Belvedere, was encouraged to fight on by Lord Beaverbrook, the owner of *Express* newspapers, and Winston Churchill. In a conversation with Noel Coward, Churchill said, 'Why shouldn't the King marry his cutie?'

'Because England does not want a Queen Cutie,' Coward replied.

On 5 December, Edward told Baldwin of his decision to abdicate. The instrument of abdication was signed on 10 December. It was witnessed by the king's three brothers. Edward's decision was conveyed to the House of Commons, who passed an Abdication Act.

Edward was allowed to make a broadcast to the nation on the following evening. No longer king, he was introduced by John Reith, the director general of the BBC, as 'His Royal Highness Prince Edward'. The former king addressed his worldwide radio audience.

'You must believe me when I tell you that I have found it impossible to carry the heavy burden of responsibility and to discharge my duties as king as I would wish to do, without the help and support of the woman I love.'

And he assured his listeners that 'the decision I have made has been mine and mine alone'.

Because the monarch was also head of the Church of England, it was made clear that it would not be appropriate for him to marry a divorcee. So the king was persuaded to abdicate rather than create a constitutional crisis. On 10 December 1936 Edward signed the Instrument of Abdication at Windsor, which was witnessed by his three brothers. Edward VIII's reign formally ceased on 11 December. Strangely enough, James II had vacated the throne on the same date in 1688. Edward had occupied the throne for 327 days. It had been the shortest reign since the time of Edward V.

Edward married Mrs Simpson in a civil ceremony at the Château de Candé,

ABOVE *The duke and duchess of Windsor caused controversy when they met the German chancellor Adolf Hitler on 23 October 1937.*

near Tour in France on 3 June 1937. The marriage produced no children and the couple spent the rest of their lives in exile, largely in France. Controversially, the duke and duchess of Windsor visited Nazi Germany in 1937, where they met Adolf Hitler. There were concerns over Edward's loyalty during the war. It was

feared that Hitler would put Edward back on the throne as his vassal if he succeeded in invading Britain. Edward certainly favoured a negotiated settlement with Germany. In order to get him out of harm's way the prime minister, Winston Churchill, appointed him governor of the Bahamas. Even there, his political insensitivity provoked riots. He quit in 1945 and the couple returned to France. After that, Edward only visited England when he had to attend the funerals of family members. In 1972 his niece Elizabeth II visited him while she was on a state visit to France. The duke of Windsor was by then nearing the end of his life – he died of throat cancer in Paris on 28 May 1972. His body was returned to England to be buried at Frogmore, within the grounds of Windsor Castle. The duchess of Windsor was buried at his side when she died in 1986.

The Reluctant King

After his abdication, Edward was succeeded by his brother Albert, duke of York, who ascended the throne as George VI (r.1936–52). He chose the name in order to associate his reign with that of his father George V. One of his first actions was to create his brother duke of Windsor. However, the king continually refused to grant the duchess of Windsor the style of Royal Highness, which remained a source of ill feeling.

George VI was the second son of George V and Mary of Teck. He was born at York Cottage, Sandringham on 14 December 1895. It was the 34th anniversary of Albert the Prince Consort's death so he was christened Albert Frederick Arthur George in his honour. Unlike his charismatic and worldly brother, George – or Bertie as he was known to the family – was a withdrawn and nervous child with a pronounced stammer. This was a great embarrassment to him and it hampered him in his royal duties. He was also made to wear splints to correct his knock-knees. His situation was worsened by being forced to write with his right hand when he was naturally left-handed.

Prince Albert was educated by a tutor at home. He later attended the Naval Colleges at Osborne and Dartmouth, where he was overshadowed by his handsome and popular elder brother. Albert was a poor student and he came bottom of the class at Osborne. Both brothers found it difficult to communicate with their father. In 1913 Albert joined the Royal Navy as a midshipman and saw action at the Battle of Jutland in the First World War. Although he suffered from seasickness, he enjoyed being away from his family and out of the public eye. He later qualified as a pilot with the Royal Naval Air Service. After the war he went to Trinity College, Cambridge, where he took an interest in constitutional history. In 1920, he was made duke of York, the traditional title of the monarch's second son.

That same year, Bertie met Lady Elizabeth Angela Marguerite Bowes-Lyon, the ninth of the ten children of Claude George Bowes-Lyon, earl of Strathmore and Kinghorne and Nina Cecilia Cavendish-Bentinck. Bertie's parents approved of Lady Elizabeth and Bertie proposed marriage, but he was turned down on two occasions. However, when he proposed for the third time he was accepted. The marriage took place at

LEFT *The prince of Wales, the future Edward VIII, shown with his brother the duke of York, who became George VI.*

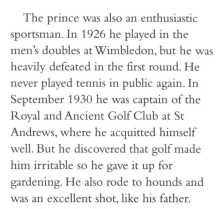

BELOW *George VI was reluctant to become king. He suffered from a debilitating stammer, but he played a pivotal role as head of state during World War II.*

OPPOSITE *King George VI and Queen Elizabeth – formerly Lady Elizabeth Bowes-Lyon – in their coronation regalia.*

Westminster Abbey on 26 April 1923 and the union produced two daughters. Princess Elizabeth Alexandra Mary – later Queen Elizabeth – was born in London in 1926 and Princess Margaret Rose – later the countess of Snowdon – was born at Glamis Castle, the Scottish seat of the Bowes-Lyon family, in 1930.

Initially the Yorks lived at White Lodge in Richmond Park, but they found it too large, expensive and public. In 1926 they moved to 145 Piccadilly and from 1931 they used Royal Lodge in Windsor Great Park as their country house.

Prince Albert became a prominent philanthropist. He was president of the Industrial Welfare Society, which made him familiar with a wide range of industrial developments while bringing him into contact with trade unionists. From 1921 to 1939 he ran the Duke of York's Camps, at which equal numbers of working-class and public-school boys enjoyed a week of games, competitions and discussions. In the 1920s – a period of social deprivation, high unemployment and class tension – these camps were seen as a bold experiment in social integration. Never before had a royal prince shown sustained interest in a cause of this sort. He was unusually relaxed and happy during his visits to the camps.

The prince was also an enthusiastic sportsman. In 1926 he played in the men's doubles at Wimbledon, but he was heavily defeated in the first round. He never played tennis in public again. In September 1930 he was captain of the Royal and Ancient Golf Club at St Andrews, where he acquitted himself well. But he discovered that golf made him irritable so he gave it up for gardening. He also rode to hounds and was an excellent shot, like his father.

Although he did not share his elder brother's enthusiasm for travel, he still visited the Balkans in 1923 and East Africa in the following year. On his return Prince Albert made the closing speech at the British Empire Exhibition in the new Wembley Stadium. Because this event was broadcast, the entire nation heard his stutter for the first time. It became clear that his speech impediment would hamper him in his duties, so professional help was obtained. From October 1926 he was treated by Lionel Logue, an Australian speech therapist. As the prince's confidence increased his stutter decreased, although it by no means disappeared. In 1927, the Yorks visited New Zealand and Australia after sailing there on HMS *Renown*. The prince was in Melbourne for Anzac day – 25 April – and he opened the new parliament building in Canberra on 9 May. His speeches on both occasions were considered great successes.

When Albert had married he had no expectation of the crown. However, as his brother's bachelorhood continued he slowly accepted the fact that one day he might become king. This was brought home to him in the winter of 1928, when his father fell dangerously ill. Had George V died, the prince of Wales would have become king and the duke of York would have become heir presumptive.

While the Yorks strongly disapproved of the twice-divorced American Mrs Simpson they were even more concerned that the king would abdicate. George VI had been educated as a simple midshipman and he was terrified of the responsibilities that had suddenly been thrust upon him.

'This is absolutely terrible, I'm quite unprepared for it,' he told Lord Louis Mountbatten. 'David has been trained for this all his life. I've never seen a state paper. I'm only a naval officer. It's the only thing I know about.'

He broke down in front of his mother and sobbed like a child. Nevertheless he shouldered the responsibility.

'You can be assured,' he said, 'that I will do my best to clear up the inevitable mess, if the whole fabric does not crumble

RIGHT *Winston Churchill was a supporter of Edward VIII during the abdication crisis, but mobilized Britain in World War II for George VI.*

under the shock and strain of it all.'

He was better prepared than he thought. His father had ensured that Prince Albert had regularly undertaken public duties, despite his shyness. He had spoken in public, made broadcasts and been filmed and photographed. His other advantages were a government with a large majority and a well-informed wife, who was happy to act as confidante. George VI was crowned in Westminster Abbey on 12 May 1937, the date planned for his brother's coronation. The ceremony was broadcast worldwide and George spoke on the radio that evening.

Like his brother, George supported the appeasement policy that Neville Chamberlain had adopted towards Germany and Italy since he had supplanted Baldwin in 1937. Freshly returned from signing the Munich Agreement with Hitler, Chamberlain even appeared on the balcony of Buckingham Palace with the king on 30 September 1938. He was still proudly proclaiming that he had brought 'peace in our time'. George then shored up the Anglo-French alliance by making a state visit in July 1938. He also forged a close personal friendship with United States president Franklin D. Roosevelt. The president was the king's host in Washington, DC and at his country home, Hyde Park, in New York State. George had just completed a state tour of Canada. It had been the first-ever visit to a dominion by a British monarch.

During the Second World War, George followed in his father's footsteps by doing all he could to boost morale. He resumed his father's practice of making a Christmas broadcast, which he had earlier discontinued. Then he visited the fleet at Invergordon and the British Expeditionary Force in France. When Chamberlain fell from power, George favoured Lord Halifax as his successor –

Halifax's wife was one of the queen's ladies-in-waiting and the couple regularly dined with the king and queen. When Halifax refused to serve, George sent for Winston Churchill and asked him to form a government.

The king and queen visited armaments factories and the blitzed areas of London, and shared in the privations of their subjects. They adhered to clothing and food rationing and made a public show of living at Buckingham Palace, even though it was bombed nine times during the war. In fact, the royal couple only remained in the palace during the day. At night they returned to the relative safety of Windsor Castle.

But in a strange way Hitler's bombing of Buckingham Palace increased the popularity of the monarchy. It raised their standing in the United States and it made royal visits to the bombed areas of London a lot easier. The appearance of the royal couple in cinema newsreels was often greeted with applause.

As Queen Elizabeth famously observed, 'I'm glad we've been bombed. We can now look the East End in the face.'

The king was so much moved by the bravery of ordinary civilians during the bombing that he introduced the George Cross and the George Medal. These were medals for heroism that could be awarded to those outside the armed forces. By the end of the war, George calculated that he had personally bestowed over 44,000 medals and decorations. Usually they were given out at the Tuesday morning investitures in Buckingham Palace. Afterwards, George would lunch with Winston Churchill in order to familiarize himself with the progress of the war. When the prime minister was away he would send telegrams to the king. George was particularly concerned that Churchill might be assassinated and regularly asked

him for his advice on a successor.

After the Axis forces had surrendered in North Africa in May 1943 the king went to visit the troops there. Travelling under the name of General Lyon he visited army camps and former battlefields, covering 6,700 miles (10,800 km) in two weeks. All of this was a big ordeal for him. He was afraid of flying and he suffered from a phobia that gave him a fear of inspecting lines of troops. It was sometimes only with difficulty that he could be persuaded to leave his tent. However, the king reported that 'the real gem of [his] tour' was his entrance into Valletta harbour, Malta on 20 June 1943. Although he was suffering from severe dysentery, he took the salute from the bridge of HMS *Aurora*. He was well received because on 15 April 1942 he had awarded the people of Malta the George Cross for their heroism during their long period of siege and bombing. He also wanted to award the citizens of Stalingrad a George Cross in recognition

ABOVE *George VI and Queen Elizabeth appeared to share the dangers of their subjects during the London Blitz, but they spent their nights in the safety of Windsor.*

ABOVE *Winston Churchill joins King George VI, Queen Elizabeth, Princess Elizabeth and Princess Margaret on the balcony of Buckingham Palace on VE Day, 8 May 1945.*

of their heroism, but this was thought to be inappropriate. A sword of honour – the personal gift of the king – was sent instead. Meanwhile George maintained cordial relations with the Americans by means of a long series of letters. Mrs Eleanor Roosevelt reciprocated by paying a visit in October 1942.

Like Churchill, the king was opposed to the D-Day landings in France, favouring renewed efforts in Italy. However, when he attended a meeting on 15 May 1944, in which senior staff officers were being briefed on the landings, he closed the proceedings with an impromptu speech praising the plan. The king then wanted to accompany the

British troops on D-Day, but he was persuaded that the risks were too great. In turn, he talked Winston Churchill out of going. Instead, King George made a broadcast to the nation on the evening of 6 June and visited the Normandy beaches ten days later. In July and August he visited the troops in Italy and in October he visited recently liberated Belgium. He had made a similar trip in 1918, but that time he had been representing his father. However, he was prevented from visiting India and the Far East.

George VI was a symbol of the nation and so he was at the centre of the VE Day (Victory in Europe) celebrations on

BELOW *Victory in World War II was celebrated at the Festival of Britain on the South Bank of the Thames in London in 1951.*

8 May 1945. Crowds packed the Mall and the royal family made repeated appearances on the balcony of Buckingham Palace, with Winston Churchill at their side. The king then broadcast to the nation. In the days that followed the king and queen drove in state through east and south London and attended services of thanksgiving at St Paul's Cathedral in London and St Giles' Cathedral in Edinburgh. On 17 May George VI made a speech in Westminster Hall to members of both houses of Parliament. At the end of his address his voice faltered as he mentioned his brother the duke of Kent, who had been killed in a plane crash in 1942. Churchill then

waved his top hat and called for three cheers for the king. It was a popular move.

George was so exhausted by the war that, fearing the worst, he asked for the Regency Act to be amended. The Regency Act of 1943 allowed his daughter Elizabeth to be included among the counsellors of state from the age of 18 onwards.

Nevertheless, he opposed the suggestion that she be made princess of Wales. As the war continued in the Far East, the king and Winston Churchill were informed of the existence of the atomic bomb and its intended use. However, the information was not shared with Clement Attlee, the Labour leader and deputy prime minister. In May 1945, with the war against Japan not yet over, the Labour Party announced its plans to withdraw from the wartime coalition, thereby forcing an election. At first George VI refused to accept Churchill's resignation, but he had no choice when the request was repeated. When Labour won the general election Clement Attlee followed the king's advice and picked Ernest Bevin as his foreign secretary. On 15 August George VI opened Parliament. That evening he appeared on the balcony of Buckingham Palace as part of the celebrations of VJ Day (Victory over Japan).

In 1947 the king's cousin, Lord Louis Mountbatten, was sent to oversee the

ABOVE *Queen Elizabeth, the Queen Mother, outlived her husband George VI by more than 50 years.*

establishment of independent republics in India, Pakistan and Burma. George VI's role as emperor of India was about to end. This did little to affect the status of the monarchy in England, where the royal family's main role was to symbolize the return to normality. The king gave his full support to the Festival of Britain, which was to be held in 1951. It was timed to coincide with the centenary of the Great Exhibition. But his health was already failing – he had undergone a major operation in 1949. By nature he was a worrier and that made him a heavy smoker. In 1951 he was diagnosed with lung cancer, although he was never told.

George VI made his final public appearance on 31 January 1952, when his daughter Elizabeth and her husband the duke of Edinburgh were leaving London Airport for a tour of Africa. It was noted that the king looked haggard as he stood waving goodbye at the airport. He died peacefully in his sleep at Sandringham House on the night of 6 February 1952. Some 300,000 people filed past his coffin while he was lying in state at Westminster Hall. On 15 February the king was placed in St George's Chapel, Windsor, where a memorial chapel was built and dedicated in 1969. When his younger daughter Princess Margaret died on 9 February 2002, after a series of strokes, her remains were cremated so they could be placed in her father's tomb. His widow Queen Elizabeth – known as the Queen Mother after her husband's death – died at the age of 101 on 30 March 2002 and was also buried with her husband at Windsor.

The New Elizabethan Age

George VI was succeeded by Elizabeth II, the eldest daughter of his marriage to Lady Elizabeth Bowes-Lyon. She was born on 21 April 1926 at 17, Bruton Street, Mayfair – the London home of

LEFT *Queen Elizabeth II, daughter of George VI, pictured here in February 1952 when she acceded to the throne.*

her maternal grandparents, Claude, earl of Strathmore and Nina Cecilia Cavendish-Bentinck. The home secretary was present at the birth, which had been the custom since James Francis Stuart had been born in 1688. It had been suggested that the infant James was not the real child of James II.

The future Elizabeth II was christened Elizabeth Alexandra Mary by the

archbishop of Canterbury – she was called Elizabeth after her mother, Mary after her grandmother, Mary of Teck, and Alexandra after her great-grandmother, Alexandra of Denmark. Elizabeth was not at first placed in the direct line of succession because it was assumed that her father's elder brother, the prince of Wales, would eventually marry and have children. However, she was a great favourite with her grandparents, George V and Queen Mary. While George was inclined to be gruff with others he doted on Lilibet, as she was known in the family. She grew up in seclusion because her education took place within the confines of the royal palaces. Her early education was provided by a Scottish governess, Miss Crawford, while her later studies were supervised by the Provost of Eton College. The abdication of her uncle had by then placed her in line to the throne so she was educated accordingly.

During the Second World War, Elizabeth was allowed to take part in National Service. She was enlisted in the Women's Auxiliary Territorial Service, where she trained as a driver. Her rank was Second Lieutenant Elizabeth Windsor. It was her first chance to mix with ordinary people outside royal circles. On VE night, 8 May 1945, Elizabeth and her sister Margaret were allowed to mingle with the crowds celebrating outside Buckingham Palace and for once they were not recognized.

Princess Elizabeth began to assume some official royal engagements when she was just a teenager. On her 21st birthday she made a speech dedicating her life to the service of her future subjects. The key to her future role would be a suitable marriage.

What was needed was another Prince Albert. Fortunately she fell for a distant cousin, Prince Philip of Greece and Denmark, who had served in the Royal Navy during the war. His surname was Schleswig-Holstein-Sonderburg-Glücksburg, but he took his mother's anglicized surname of Mountbatten. When he became naturalized as a British subject his prospective father-in-law created him duke of Edinburgh and granted him royal status. Elizabeth and Philip were married at Westminster

PRINCE PHILIP

Philip Schleswig-Holstein-Sonderburg-Glücksburg was born on 10 June 1921 at the Villa Mon Repos, Corfu. The family was soon forced into exile and his parents drifted apart. His mother, who was deaf, suffered a severe breakdown, while his father adopted a playboy lifestyle in Monaco. Philip was brought up under the direction of his maternal uncle, Lord Louis Mountbatten. He was educated at Gordonstoun in Scotland and later entered Dartmouth Naval College.

Princess Elizabeth met and fell in love with the blond and handsome Prince Philip of Greece before the end of the Second World War but her father, George VI, would not immediately consent to his daughter's marriage. He liked Philip but he doubted that his daughter's affections would remain fixed on the first man she had viewed in a romantic light. The couple were separated when Elizabeth accompanied her parents and her sister on a tour of South Africa in 1947, but on her return it was clear that her feelings for Philip had remained unchanged. At that point her father at last agreed to the couple's engagement.

Thanks to the intricate web of genealogy that is a feature of Europe's royal houses, Philip is Elizabeth's cousin twice over. Both are descended from Queen Victoria, as are many other royals. Philip is the son of Prince Andrew of Greece and Denmark and Princess Alice of Battenberg. The royal houses of Greece and Denmark became linked when the Danish Oldenburg dynasty was invited to take up the throne of Greece. Prince Philip's mother was the granddaughter of another Princess Alice, the second daughter of Queen Victoria, who had been married to Louis, Grand Duke of Hesse, which meant that the couple were third cousins by virtue of their shared English descent. They are also second cousins once removed because of their shared descent from the house of Denmark. The queen's great-grandmother, Alexandra of Denmark, was the sister of Philip's grandfather, Prince William of Denmark, who later became George I of Greece.

The match between Philip and Elizabeth was not without its controversy. For a start, Philip was brought up in the Greek Orthodox Church. He had no money and his sisters had married prominent Nazi supporters. One of them had married an SS officer who was an aide to Heinrich Himmler. It was even reported that the Queen Mother was against the marriage. However, the nation, the Commonwealth and the world craved romance and spectacle after the devastation of the Second World War.

Wartime rationing was still in force at that time so Princess Elizabeth had to come up with enough coupons to buy the material for her gown. When they married in Westminster Abbey on 20 November 1947, the couple received over 2,500 wedding gifts from around the world. The wedding was seen as the first glimmer of postwar prosperity.

MONARCHY IN THE TELEVISION AGE

When the coronation took place in Westminster Abbey on 2 June 1953, Queen Elizabeth requested that the entire ceremony, with the exception of the anointing and the communion, be televised and shown throughout the Commonwealth. It was watched by an estimated 20 million people. She wore a gown commissioned from the couturier Norman Hartnell, which featured the embroidered floral emblems of the countries of the Commonwealth: the Tudor rose of England, the thistle of Scotland, the Welsh leek, the Irish shamrock, the Australian wattle flower, the maple leaf of Canada, the New Zealand fern, the protea of South Africa, the lotus flowers of India and Ceylon and Pakistan's wheat, cotton and jute.

The new queen followed her father's practice of making a radio broadcast at Christmas. From 1957 onwards the queen could also be seen on the television screen. Television had grown apace by 1969 – the investiture of the prince of Wales at Caernarfon Castle was watched by an estimated 200 million people worldwide.

ABOVE *Queen Elizabeth's annual Christmas message to her subjects in the UK and the Commonwealth has become an institution.*

In the same year a more informal film showing the royal family off duty was watched by some 23 million people. There were fears that royalty would be demystified in the process. Nevertheless, the queen was again shown in some of her more unguarded moments in the BBC documentary *Elizabeth R,* which was broadcast in 1992. In 2007 another documentary, *A Year With The Queen,* caused a furore when it apparently showed the queen storming out of a photo shoot set up by *Vanity Fair* photographer Annie Leibovitz. But the footage had been spliced together out of sequence.

In public relations terms, the royal image derived more benefit from the 2006 feature film *The Queen,* in which the monarch was shown struggling with the aftermath of the death of Princess Diana. Helen Mirren, the actress who played the queen in the film, won an Oscar for her portrayal.

Abbey on 20 November 1947. In 1949, they took up residence in Clarence House. Because Prince Philip was still a serving naval officer they lived intermittently in Malta, where he had been posted. The first child of the marriage was Prince Charles Philip Arthur George of Edinburgh, later prince of Wales, who was born on 14 November 1948. A few weeks later the king issued letters patent granting Elizabeth's children royal status. As the offspring of a mere duke they would otherwise have occupied a lower position. A second child, Anne Elizabeth Alice Louise, later created Princess Royal, arrived on 15 August 1950. By this time, the king's health was deteriorating so Elizabeth and her husband took on royal duties and official tours on his behalf. They visited Greece, Italy and Malta and toured Canada. In 1951 they visited United

States president Harry S. Truman in Washington, DC. On that trip, Elizabeth carried a draft Accession Declaration, in case the king should die while she was out of the United Kingdom.

Elizabeth and Philip went on tour again in the following year. In 1952 they were in a remote part of Kenya when George VI died. It fell to Prince Philip to inform Princess Elizabeth of her father's death. She was proclaimed queen of Canada on the 6 February 1952. The British proclamation was read in St James's Palace on the following day. Under the new constitutional arrangements, the countries of the British Empire that retained the monarch as head of state had to proclaim her accession individually. The formal abandonment of the indivisibility of the crown was confirmed by statute in 1953. Instead, the new title 'Head of the Commonwealth' was conferred on the queen, in recognition of the republican status of India, Pakistan and other Commonwealth countries.

At the insistence of Elizabeth's grandmother, Queen Mary, it was announced that the queen and her heirs should continue to be known as the house of Windsor. In that way the name of the dynasty founded by George V would be perpetuated. This annoyed Prince Philip, who wanted the family name changed to Mountbatten. He is reported to have exclaimed angrily, 'I'm a bloody amoeba!'

In 1960 a further declaration regarding the family surname was issued by the queen. It stated that while she and her heirs would continue to be known as the house of Windsor, any descendants not inheriting the throne would take the surname Mountbatten-Windsor. In fact, all of the queen's children have used that surname as a courtesy to their father. After Elizabeth took the throne, she

gave birth to two more children – Prince Andrew Albert Christian Edward, later created duke of York, who was born on 19 February 1960, and Prince Edward Anthony Richard Louis, later earl of Wessex, who was born on 10 March 1964.

While the reign of Elizabeth II was vaunted as a 'new Elizabethan age, the British Empire was being rapidly dismantled. However, a large number of former colonies retained the queen as head of state. In theory, Elizabeth II rules over some 130 million people, but she is represented by governor-generals at a local level and rarely interferes in political matters.

Prince Philip has attempted to modernize the monarchy. He began by reorganizing the royal household and then in 1956 he went on to make his own contribution by instituting the Duke of Edinburgh's Award scheme. Next, the public were allowed to see previously hidden items from the royal art collection. In 1962 a number of items were put on display in the Queen's Gallery, a bomb-damaged chapel in Buckingham Palace. A significant gesture towards royal informality was made in 1970, when the royal couple introduced the 'walkabout' during a visit to Australia and New Zealand.

The queen has continued to take an interest in her overseas role. Between 1953 and 1954 she went on a six-month round the world tour, accompanied by Prince Philip. This made her the first monarch to circumnavigate the globe. She also became the first reigning monarch of Australia, New Zealand and Fiji to visit those nations. In 1957, she made a state visit to the United States as queen of Canada. After addressing the United Nations General Assembly she returned to Canada to open its parliament, the first monarch of Canada to do so. Two years later, she was back in the United States where she met President Dwight D. Eisenhower. Then in 1961 she visited Turkey and toured India, Iran, Pakistan and Nepal for the first time. Thirty years later, in 1991, she became the first British monarch to address a joint session of the United States Congress. Other 'firsts' followed. In 2005 she was the first Canadian monarch to address the Legislative Assembly of Alberta and in 2007 she became the first British monarch to address the Virginia General Assembly. Throughout her reign Queen Elizabeth has visited virtually every Commonwealth country and has attended nearly every Commonwealth Heads of Government Meeting, making her the most widely travelled head of state in history.

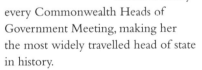

ABOVE *Prince Charles and Diana, princess of Wales, on the steps of St Paul's Cathedral on their wedding day, 29 July 1981.*

Queen Elizabeth celebrated her Silver Jubilee in 1977 and her Golden Jubilee in 2002. Five years later, she celebrated her 60th wedding anniversary. At the time of writing she is the third longest reigning monarch of England, after Queen Victoria and George III.

The behaviour of some of the younger members of her family has often provoked criticism of the monarchy. Princess Anne's marriage to Captain Mark Phillips in 1973 ended in divorce in 1992. Since the Church of England did not allow divorcees to remarry in its churches, while the Church of Scotland did, the Princess Royal married her second husband, Commander Timothy Laurence, at Crathie Kirk, near the Queen's Balmoral estate in Aberdeenshire.

Scandal surrounded the collapse of the marriage of Prince Andrew, duke of York to Sarah Ferguson. The tabloids had published revealing photographs of the duchess of York. She had been caught topless and in compromising positions with her financial adviser, John Bryan. Meanwhile the marriage of the prince of Wales to Lady Diana Spencer in July 1981 had run into difficulties. Ill-matched from the outset, both partners had engaged in extramarital affairs. Their marriage had become little more than a façade that was being maintained for the sake of their public image. The whole sordid story was exposed in the book *Diana: Her True Story* by Andrew Morton. After that, Prince Charles and Princess Diana made separate television appearances in an attempt to generate public sympathy. However, Princess Diana's *Panorama* appearance was a bridge too far. She not only admitted her involvement in Morton's book but also an affair with an army officer, Major James Hewitt. The queen advised the couple to divorce for the sake of their children and the monarchy, which could be irreparably damaged. The marriage ended on 28 August 1996.

When Princess Diana died in a car accident in Paris on 31 August 1997, the Prince of Wales and the royal family came under criticism. They were accused of being cold and unfeeling and out of tune with the mood of the nation when they failed to respond to the tragedy. The queen has since striven to alter those perceptions. Now in her eighties, she is widely admired for the dedicated and dutiful manner with which she has carried out her often difficult role.

The Future of the British Monarchy

Many people imagine that Prince Charles or one of his sons will automatically become England's monarch after the death of Queen Elizabeth, but the reality of the situation is more complex. The monarchy enjoys a widespread popularity with many British residents and tourists alike, and arguably plays a role in maintaining a sense of national identity, but is that enough? A royal family, with all its traditions and ceremony, sometimes seems out of step with a complex modern society like ours.

Since the queen came to the throne in 1952 a number of Commonwealth countries have dropped her as head of state. In 1999 Australia held a referendum on the subject of whether or not it should become a republic. Roughly 55 per cent of the voting population wanted to maintain the monarchy. However, it is likely that sooner or later the vote will go the other way because younger people, in Britain as well as Australia, tend to have anti-monarchist views.

It can be argued that the monarchy has served England, Britain and the world well – particularly since the Glorious Revolution, with its accompanying constitutional constraints. But it would be very difficult to argue for the establishment of a monarchy in Britain, if such a thing did not exist.

In the past, when kings and queens had a much larger influence on government, some societies have seized power only to find that the monarchy was more difficult to replace than they thought. For instance, in the 17th century the confusion after the beheading of Charles I was only resolved when Oliver Cromwell became king in all but name. The French were little better off after their revolution in 1789. They soon found themselves ruled by an emperor, Napoleon I, followed by a series of disastrous kings.

Even though Britain restored the monarchy after the Civil War, the conflict still paved the way to many of the civil liberties that we enjoy today. The whole question of Britain's present and future constitution was discussed during the Putney Debates of 1647, when members of the victorious New Model Army and the radical Levellers held a series of discussions in St Mary's Church in Putney. These debates provided many of the ideas and much of the wordage that went into the American Declaration of Independence and the United States Constitution. The American system of government, with its bicameral Congress and its separate executive president, is closely based on its British equivalent. There is one important difference – the Americans do not, of course, have a monarchy. America's example has been followed by many other countries around the world. Perhaps one day Britain might join them? On the other hand…

BELOW *The Prince of Wales with Prince William (left) and Prince Harry on the balcony of Buckingham Palace on 4 August 2000.*

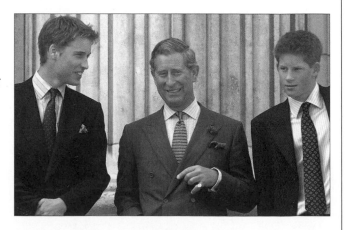

INDEX

PICTURE CREDITS

Clipart.com: 13, 14 (bottom), 22, 24, 25, 32, 33, 34, 38, 55, 58, 66, 67, 84 (2), 98, 105 (bottom), 116 (top), 117, 119, 129 (bottom), 133, 137 (top), 146 (top), 184; Corbis: 94, 180, 202, 204, 205; Dover: 59; Mary Evans Picture Library: 6, 10, 17, 23, 19, 28, 35, 37, 44, 45, 46, 47, 50, 53, 56, 57, 62, 68, 72 (top), 73, 75, 76, 78, 79, 86, 89, 92, 96, 110, 113, 120, 124 (4), 126, 127, 134, 136, 138, 139 (left), 142 (2), 146 (top), 149 (bottom), 150, 151, 152 (bottom), 157, 159 (2), 167 (2), 168, 171 (bottom), 176, 178, 183 (bottom), 185, 186, 187, 188, 189, 190, 191, 193, 194, 196, 197, 198, 199, 200; Photos.com: 36, 40, 48, 52, 54, 61, 63, 64, 65, 69, 70, 71 (2), 74, 80, 81, 82, 83, 85, 88 (2), 90, 91, 95, 97, 99, 100 (right), 101, 104, 107 (bottom), 111, 118, 122, 123, 128, 130, 135, 137 (bottom), 139 (right), 141, 143, 146 (bottom right), 152 (top), 153, 154, 158, 161, 162, 163, 169, 170 (left), 172, 173, 174 (2), 182; Rebecca Glover: 12, 14 (top), 26; Shutterstock: 30, 39, 41; TopFoto: 43, 195.